1

HISTORICAL COMPUTING
Volume II

PROGRAMMING STATISTICS IN *BASIC*

BY

DR. Peta Trigger Ph.D, Ed.D (Lon)

Northampton Academy of Post Doctoral Studies

K B P

2 Emms Hill Barns

Hamsterley

County Durham

First published 2014

ISBN 9781495399121

PRINTED BY CREATESPACE

https://www.createspace.com

FOREWORD

This volume is principally concerned with how 'old fashioned' *BASIC* (not to be confused with more modern programming media such as Visual Basic) may be used to computerise the statistical tests described in Siegel's book *Nonparametric statistics for the behavioural sciences,* originally achieved by the author in the early 1980's. Some of these tests were used in her Ph.D research, and examples have been drawn from this, where applicable. Although Siegel outlines the rationale and types of data suitable for each test, all his examples are worked by hand. Naturally enough, for the purpose of illustration small groups of data with convenient values were used for the most part so as not to obscure the method by tedious calculation.

So, to facilitate their use and avoid long-winded and error prone calculation with larger data sets with any realistic values, this author decided write the procedures involved as statements in *BASIC*. As noted in Volume I of this series, *BASIC* is an easy to use and versatile programming language and, with a particularly helpful debugging facility, enables the programmer to concentrate more effort on translating the statistical method into the logic of program construction and less on nuances of syntax and problems of program execution.

Whilst it is true that *BASIC* is an interpreted language in which statements are executed line by line, which therefore suffers a speed disadvantage in comparison with compiled languages where the entire program is converted into machine code before execution, this may only be serious where the statistical test involves long, oft-repeated mathematical procedures on large data sets (for example in the Randomization tests described in Chapter 5). Even where this is the case, *BASIC* still facilitates the writing of a program which will run as intended, and once this is achieved, the logic used can be transferred to a faster, and more complex, compiled language environment if need be.

The *BASIC* programs included here were at first written for the 1984 *Amstrad PCW8256* 'micro-computer' and subsequently transferred to Notepad in *Windows Vista* for use on *Windows* computers.

In the process I have used the opportunity to develop the programs further, for example by extending them to cater for larger samples, incorporating corrections to test statistics for ties in ranked data and adding look-up tables of critical values of test statistics. This involved much re-typing, and inevitably errors were made in copying the *BASIC* files. However the program *Vintbas* (Kopnicky (2011)) downloaded from the www provides a good editor for debugging which identifies any lines of the program containing errors and the error type, and even gives an indication as to whereabouts in a line the error is located.

There were a few, but important, differences between *Vintbas* and the *Locomotive BASIC* in which the statistical test programs were originally written, which in one or two instances were discovered only after painstaking search, trial and re-trial in looking for the source of error in the output of the program affected. Usually, the offending instruction was located by checking the values the variables involved in the calculations in the program by inserting print variable:stop statements into the program, and comparing these with those of the original program on an *Amstrad PCW8256* kept running at the same time.

TABLE OF CONTENTS

CHAPTER NUMBERS, HEADINGS AND PAGE NUMBERS

8. APPENDICES

8

LIST OF TABLES

LIST OF FIGURES

1. INTRODUCTION

Following Siegel (1956), non-parametric tests will be classified by: 'level of measurement' (nominal, ordinal or interval); whether the samples are related or independent; number of samples (one, two or k-sample case); and measures of correlation. This will be followed by a discussion of the various levels of measurement possible in data; relationship between samples; and numbers of samples. But we begin with an introduction to 'non-parametric' statistics and their use. Chapter I concludes with a table listing the tests covered in this book and their classification.

Non-parametric Tests and their Use

Non-parametric tests are typically used where one or more of the following apply to the data to which a statistical test is to be applied:

(1) the data cannot be relied to be a sample from a normal distributed population;

(2) samples to be compared are drawn from populations which do not have the same variance;

(3) the data may be ranked or merely categorised - but numerically, for the purposes of statistical test

calculations, *differences* between them are either equivalent (categorical data) or are differences in rank (ordinal data); the *size* of these differences is not quantifiable.

Where assumptions of normality, equal variance and quantifiable distances between data *are* all met, parametric tests such as the t-test are preferred, which, because such tests make use of the extra information available in such data, constitute a more *powerful* means of hypothesis testing, which is the purpose of statistical testing. The concept of test power is considered below.

Test Power, hypothesis testing & 1- and 2-sided tests

Statistical tests are usually employed to decide whether a null hypothesis (H_0) can be rejected in favour of an alternative hypothesis (H_1) on the evidence of the data. For example, in comparing the performance of two samples of testees A and B , H_0 might be that their median scores μ_A and μ_B are equal; H_1 that $\mu_A > \mu_B$. This is known as a *one-sided* test which is applicable where the direction of difference between μ_A and μ_B can be predicted ***in*** *advance*, and can result in a greater likelihood that H_0 will be rejected. In a *two-sided* test the direction of difference is not predicted, and so in the above context H_1 is that $\mu_A \neq \mu_B$.

The *power* of a test **is the probability of rejecting the null hypothesis when it is false**, and clearly this should be as high as possible. For the reasons given above, non-parametric tests tend to have a lower power than parametric tests, and although the ability of a non-parametric test to reject the null hypothesis when it is false may be made equal to that of an equivalent parametric test (given that appropriate assumptions are met by the data) by suitably increasing sample size, very often non-parametric tests are chosen precisely *because* the sample size is small.

Degrees of freedom

This is an appropriate place to make a brief note about degrees of freedom, since the degrees of freedom and knowing how to calculate it, though simple, is important in choosing the correct value of the test statistic from statistical tables in books (such as the appendices in Siegel) or electronic media (such as graphics calculators like the *Casio Ti83*). *Degrees of freedom* refers to the number of data values which are allowed to vary depending on the data organization appropriate to the test applied. For example, if the data organization appropriate to the test is a 2 rows x 3 columns ('*contingency*') table, with entries the frequencies of data in each of the six categories, if the row and column totals represent fixed numbers of data values, it is clear that once the frequencies in one row and two columns are entered, the remaining frequencies are predetermined. Hence, in this case, there are (3-1) x (2-1) = 2 degrees of freedom, and the value of the test statistic associated with this number of degrees of freedom would be obtained from the look-up table appropriate to the test in comparing the calculated value from the data as a means of deciding whether to reject or accept the null hypothesis. More of this will be said when we come to consider applications of the tests covered to specific examples.

2. MEASUREMENT LEVELS, SAMPLES AND TESTS

Measurement Levels

The data to which statistical tests may be applied constitute a nominal, ordinal, interval or ratio scale of measurement, increasing in strength in that order in terms of the amount of information each datum carries in relation to each other datum in the sample.

Nominal or categorical data may only be sorted into one of several classes. Each of these classes is equivalent in the sense that, statistically, no one class is 'higher' or 'lower' than another. An example is the numbering of houses in the streets of a locality: all houses with the same number in the locality are equivalent in this context. Nominal data are the most restricted in terms of the statistical tests which may be used on them, being limited to those involving only equivalence operations in the calculation of their test statistic.

Ordinal or ranked data can be arranged from statistically low to high (or equal), but it cannot be said on the strength of the information in the data *how much* higher or lower a datum is in relation to another datum in the sample. An example is the honours classification of university degrees. A second class degree is higher than a third class degree but lower than a first class degree, but it cannot be said on this basis how much higher or lower a given class of degree is than any other. Data of this type are less restrictive of the statistical tests which are appropriate for use with them than is nominal data, because they can be used with tests which rank or classify the data in the procedure used in calculating the test statistic. However, ordinal or ranked data cannot be used with tests based on calculations utilizing gradations of difference between ranks. Arithmetical operations on the data values themselves, rather than on their ranks in relation to the other data in the sample, fall into the latter category.

Interval data can not only be ordered like ordinal data but it can be said how much higher or lower a datum is in comparison with any other datum in the sample. For example, in a sample of data consisting of resistances with values in Ω, in processing the data use can be made of the difference between a 47Ω resistor and 22Ω resistor that is 4Ω more than that between a 68Ω resistor and a 47Ω resistor in arithmetical operations on those data values. And so tests which classify, rank or use interval differences between data can be used with this type of data, which is therefore the least restrictive of the three data types in terms of the range of statistical tests which can be applied to the data.

Ratio data represent the highest level of measurement and is included for the sake of completeness. Because ratio data do not feature in any of the tests or comparisons between tests considered here, it will be considered only very briefly. Ratio data are based on a scale with zero at its origin. For example, length measurements form a ratio scale. This means that not only can differences between data values be compared numerically, but also the data values themselves, adding to the information content present in interval data. So there are tests in addition to those applicable to interval data, which are applicable only to ratio data.

Samples

Number of samples

Siegel classifies the number of samples to which a statistical test is to be applied as one sample, two samples or k-sample cases.

In the one sample case, the investigator is interested in comparing the data set with some distribution. For example, the interest might be in whether the attitudes expressed by a sample of respondents in categories of 'agree', 'undecided' and 'disagree' differ from a distribution with equal numbers of response in each category.

In the two-sample case, the interest is in whether two samples differ on some characteristic. For example, one might be interested in whether the two samples of testees differ from one another in their scores on a test. This the scenario on p. 41.

Finally, it may be desired to compare more than two (k-) samples . For example, the samples may be three groups of individuals aesthetically rating several types of tower construction supporting a wind turbine- lattice, concrete 'telescopic', steel tubular, etc. (p. 50).

Relatedness of samples

<u>Independent Samples</u>

Samples may be independent or related. Clearly, independence applies only in the 2- and k-sample cases; it makes no sense to speak of the independence of a single sample. In essence, independent samples may be randomly drawn from populations by assigning numbers to each individual and picking these blindly 'out of a hat' to go into each sample in turn. So if there are four samples, the first number drawn goes into Sample A, the next into Sample B, the next into Sample C and the 4th into Sample D. The fifth goes into Sample A, and so on until the pool of individuals is exhausted. The numbers in each group need not be necessarily be equal.

Another method of achieving independence in samples if one is interested in comparing the effectiveness of several methods on some aspect of behaviour, is to randomly assign each method to a group of subjects. Essentially, this would involve numbering each method and picking these out of hat (the contents of which are such that the probability of picking any one method is the same as any other), assigning the method drawn to each subject in turn.

Related Samples

Two or more groups may be related by matching them on one or more attributes or by using the same sample repeatedly (the latter is known as *'repeated measures'*). Related samples are preferred to independent samples because, where the interest is in the effect of some condition or method observed differences between samples may be due to extraneous factors rather than the experimental condition or method itself. For example, in comparing the effectiveness of several methods of instruction, extraneous factors might include general ability (intelligence), achievement motivation and previous education, any and all of which might be responsible for the difference observed. One way of mitigating this problem is to arrange for subjects who are similar in terms of these extraneous factors to be allocated to each method or condition.

Difficulties which arise in matching samples in this way are problems in assessing individuals on each extraneous factor and in including all such factors.

A surer approach is therefore to use the same subjects and apply each condition or method to each subject after a suitable time interval in a repeated measures design. The problem of improvement in performance carrying over from one method to another can be mitigated by randomly assigning the time order in which each is applied.

However, the situation being studied may make it unamenable to matching the samples or using the same sample repeatedly. For example, the extraneous factors which affect the outcome may be unknown, or differences due to methods subsequently applied to the same subject may be influenced by the application of previous methods. In such cases, independent samples have to be used.

Tests

The foregoing discussion suggests that measurement levels and number of samples are hierachical in nature, with levels of measurement becoming more sophisticated in going from nominal to ordinal to interval and ratio data. This will be reflected in the complexity of the procedures used in tests appropriate for use on data at each of these levels. The same is true of the number of samples, a test appropriate for k samples will in general entail a more involved procedure than for 2 samples, and 2 samples more than one.

Measures of correlation are included in the table as tests, since they provide a statistic with which the null hypothesis of no association between samples on some characteristic may be tested.

The description of the tests covered in this book will be ordered in accordance with the above deliberations, as laid out in the following table:

Level of Measure	Nominal (Chapter 3)	Ordinal (Chapter 4)	Interval (Chapter 5)
One sample	Binomial; Chi-square tests	Kolmogorov -Smirnov; Runs tests	
Two Sample:	Contingency Correlation test*	Spearman Correlation test*	
Independent	Chi-square; Fisher Exact tests	Median; Mann-Whitney; tests	Randomiz-ation test (independent)
Related	McNemar test	Sign; Wilcoxon; tests	Randomiz-ation test (matched pairs)
K-Sample:		Kendal Concord-ance test*	
Independent	Chi-square test	Kruskal-Wallis 1-way ANOVAR	
Related	Cochran Q test	Friedman 2-way ANOVAR	

Table 1: Layout of Tests covered in this book
* The correlation tests are placed here because it is the precisely the independence/ or relatedness of the samples that is being tested

And so the first of the next three chapters of this book is concerned with the computerisation of non-parametric tests (in *BASIC)* for use with nominal data; Chapter 4 is concerned with the computerisation of non-parametric tests for use with ordinal data, and Chapter 5 is concerned with the computerisation of non-parametric tests for use with interval data. In each case the statistical rationale of the test will be outlined, followed by a brief description of how the procedure has been programmed. If the reader has read Volume I of this series and followed the miscellaneous examples in it, he or she will be in good position to follow the logic of the main features of the programs presented here. An example of the use of each test is given which is drawn from the author's use of non-parametric tests in her Ph.D research, where appropriate. Other examples have been selected on the basis of the author's interest in electricity generation (recent books on which include Trigger (2013a,b)).

3. TESTS PROGRAMMED FOR NOMINAL DATA

One sample

<u>Binomial test</u>

Here, the data are frequencies in one of two categories representing two populations. The probability that a sample from one population will contain x data and the other N-x data, where N is the frequency in both categories combined is given by:

$$^nC_x \, P^x \cdot (1-P)^{N-x}$$

Where P is the proportion of data expected in one of the categories and

$$^nC_x = \sum_{n=1}^{x} \frac{N!}{x!(N-x)!}$$

The purpose of the test is to use this formula to test the null hypothesis that the frequencies in the two populations occur with probability P and 1-P, respectively.

The first part of the program on p. 131 prints out a 2 x 2 contingency table of observed and expected frequencies entered by the user. The factorials in nCx are calculated using a subroutine at the end of the program. But the value of nCx becomes very large as n increases, until when n is about 33 it causes an overflow (an attempt to process a number which is too large to cope with). However a good normal approximation may be used when n>33, and this features on line 210. The probability associated with value of z returned by the program can then be ascertained from tables of the standard normal distribution with mean=1 and variance=0.

However, useful criteria are that $|z|>=1.96$ is significant at the 0.05 level and $|z|>= 2.33$ at the 0.01 level.

The test is one-sided.

Example

A manufacturer claims a failure rate of 7% for its components. In a sample batch of 30, 5 components failed. The hypotheses to be tested are:

H_0: $P=P_0$

H_1: $P>P_0$

28

where $P_0 = 0.07$ (7%) and P is the observed proportion which failed.

In this case, the interest is in the probability of failure of up to 5 components under the null hypothesis.

The expected number of failures (expected frequency in category 1) is 0.07 x 30 = 2, so the frequency in category 2 is 30-2 = 28. The corresponding observed frequencies are 5 and 25 respectively.

Entering these values produces the following output from the program:

```
run_debug_basic_programs
Microsoft Windows [Version 6.0.6001]
Copyright (c) 2006 Microsoft Corporation.  All rights reserved

c:\users\pejt4\Basic_programs>bintest.bas
ENTER THE OBSERVED FREQUENCY IN CATEGORY 1? 5
ENTER THE EXPECTED FREQUENCY IN CATEGORY 1? 2
ENTER THE OBSERVED FREQUENCY IN CATEGORY 2? 25
ENTER THE EXPECTED FREQUENCY IN CATEGORY 2? 28
FIND PROBABILITY THAT >= 5 EXPECTED PRESS [1]
FIND PROBABILITY THAT <= 5 EXPECTED PRESS [2]? 2
THE CONTINGENCY TABLE OF FREQUENCIES IS:


                  OBSERVED        EXPECTED

CATEGORY 1        5               2
CATEGORY 2        25              28

TOTAL             30              30


P= .03344232
```

Since P<0.05, at the conventional 0.05 level of

significance, the null hypothesis can be rejected in favour of the alternative hypothesis that the failure rate is greater than 7%.

Chi-square One Sample Test

Here, the data are frequencies in two or more categories in a population, and the chi-square test tests whether there is a significant difference between observed frequencies in each category and that expected under the null hypothesis of no difference. H_0 is tested using the formula

$$\sum_{i=1}^{n} \frac{(O_i - E_i)^2}{E_i}$$

where n is the number of categories, O_i is the observed frequency in category i and E_i is the expected frequency in category i.

Referring to Table 1, it can be seen that the chi-square test appears for all of the (independent) one sample, two sample and k sample cases for nominal data. In essence the test is no different in each case and so the same program may be used throughout by including the ability to deal with m samples, where m can range from 1 to k. That part of the program which is concerned with the one sample case will be considered first, and the test will be revisited with added explanation in the following sections in this chapter when tests appropriate to 2 sample and k sample nominal data are considered.

A print-out of the program is on p. 132. The lines of DATA are critical values of χ^2 from tables for the significance levels 0.1, 0.05 and 0.01 with from 1-30 degrees of freedom. The program first prints out a table of observed and expected values, and line 1120 calculates the value of χ^2 from the data. Line 230 picks up the one sample case which directs program execution to a block of lines beginning at line 860 which requires the user to enter the observed numbers in each category. (Lines 240-850 which are for the two and k sample case have been omitted for clarity). Lines 1110-1130 set the number of decimal places to which the chi-square is quoted. The last part of the program assigns significance levels from the read-in data.

The test is 2-sided.

<u>Example</u>

Consider the YouGov/Sunday Times poll of 1930 GB adults on 7-8th February 2013. The poll asked respondents, "Thinking about providing for Britain's future energy generation needs, which of the following do you support the MOST?"

The results obtained were:

Nuclear power   502

Wind power   347

Wave/tidal power 347

There are 3 categories, and the proportions in each category under the null hypothesis will be set equal, giving expected frequencies of 398, 399 and 399 when rounded to the nearest whole number. The alternative hypothesis is that GB adults do show preferences in their support for the three kinds of energy generation, i.e., that the frequencies in each category and the proportions of responses in each category are not equal. The corresponding output of the program is shown below:

```
run_debug_basic_programs
ENTER THE OBSERVED FREQUENCY IN CATEGORY 1
? 502
ENTER THE EXPECTED FREQUENCY IN CATEGORY 1
? 398
ENTER THE OBSERVED FREQUENCY IN CATEGORY 2
? 347
ENTER THE EXPECTED FREQUENCY IN CATEGORY 2
? 399
ENTER THE OBSERVED FREQUENCY IN CATEGORY 3
? 347
ENTER THE EXPECTED FREQUENCY IN CATEGORY 3
? 399




THE CONTINGENCY TABLE OF FREQUENCIES IS;

CATEGORY        OBSERVED        EXPECTED

1               502             398
2               347             399
3               347             399
--------------------------------------------
      TOTAL     1196            1196

CHI-SQUARE= 40.73
  2 DEGREE(S) OF FREEDOM
H(0):P<0.01
```

Since P<0.01, the null hypothesis can be rejected in favour of the alternative hypothesis that support amongst GB adults for nuclear, wind, and wave/tidal power is unequal (Support for nuclear power appears to be greater than for wind or wave/tidal power)..

Two samples

Chi-square Two Samples Test for Independent Samples

H_0 is tested using the formula

$$\sum_{i=1}^{n} \sum_{j=1}^{2} \frac{(O_i - E_i)^2}{E_i}$$

In the resulting n x 2 contingency table, the expected frequencies in each cell are calculated by multiplying the row total by the column total and then dividing by the grand total. This is done beginning on lines 510-530 in the computer program for this test which is shown on pp. 134-6.

The degrees of freedom are:
(number of categories-1) x (number of samples -1)

calculated at line 840.

The program also contains lines added to the program for the chi-square one sample test to cope with a second sample (lines 245-850).

<u>Example</u>

In a questionnaire survey, Trigger (1985) found that 14 teachers of the normally hearing out of 17 taught Advanced Level mathematics, compared with 3 out of 22 teachers of the hearing-impaired. The null hypothesis was that proportions of teachers of the normally hearing and hearing-impaired teaching Advanced Level mathematics are equal. The alternative hypothesis was that they are not equal. The output of the program using using this data is shown below:

```
run_debug_basic_programs
ENTER THE NUMBER OF CATEGORIES? 2
ENTER THE FREQUENCY IN CATEGORY 1 SAMPLE 1
? 14
ENTER THE FREQUENCY IN CATEGORY 1 SAMPLE 2
? 3
ENTER THE FREQUENCY IN CATEGORY 2 SAMPLE 1
? 3
ENTER THE FREQUENCY IN CATEGORY 2 SAMPLE 2
? 19




                       SAMPLE
              1          2                    TOTAL (O/E)
CATEGORY
      1 O             14        3          17
      1 E             7.4102564 9.589744   17

      2 O             3         19         22
      2 E             9.589744  12.410256  22

         TOTAL (O/E) 17        22          39


                              O: OBSERVED FREQUENCY
                              E: EXPECTED FREQUENCY

    CHI-SQUARE= 15.727099

    H(0):P<0.01
```

Since P<0.01, the null hypothesis was rejected in favour of the alternative hypothesis that the proportions of teachers of the normally hearing and hearing impaired teaching Advanced Level mathematics are not equal. The data suggested that a higher proportion of teachers of the normally hearing than teachers of the hearing-impaired taught mathematics at Advanced Level.

Contingency Correlation Test

The contingency correlation test is a test of association between two samples, each comprising data on *one characteristic*. Each characteristic comprises one, two, three, or more categories. The test statistic is contingency coefficient C which is calculated using the formula:

$$C = \sqrt{\frac{\chi^2}{N + \chi^2}}$$

where χ^2 is the value computed in the two-sample chi-square test and N is the total number of data. To calculate χ^2 the two sample chi-square program can be adapted to allow for data in two sets of categories, by changing the two 'samples' to the k categories of a 'set' for one characteristic, where k can be any value, the 'categories' of the 2-sample χ^2 test constituting the set for the other characteristic. This simply involves changes which allow for the variable M in the program to take any value.

The significance of C is just the significance of the associated χ^2 value. Additional lines evaluate the above expression for C. The program to calculate the contingency coefficient, determine its significance and produce a decision as to whether to reject the null hypothesis is shown in the print-out on p. 137. The test is 2-sided.

Example

The data shown in Table 2 below were collected by the author in 1982. She approached colleges of F.E. in England about the qualifications of teachers and the levels to which they taught maths:

Level/ Qualification	Certificate	Diploma	Degree
Basic Maths	17	6	5
C.S.E.	8	13	10
'O' Level	10	12	13
'A' Level	8	9	14

Table 2: Qualifications of Teachers in F.E. teaching 3 levels of Mathematics

Thus the 3 categories in data set 1 are teachers' qualifications and the 4 data set 2 categories are teaching levels.

The null hypothesis was that there is no association between teachers' levels of qualifications in maths and the levels up to which they taught the subject. The alternative and directional hypothesis was that teachers with higher qualifications in maths taught the subject to higher levels.

Entering the frequencies in Table 2 into the program produced the following input and output:

```
run_debug_basic_programs - CONTINGENCY.BAS
c:\users\pejt4\Basic_programs>CONTINGENCY.BAS
ENTER THE NUMBER OF CATEGORIES IN SET 1? 3
ENTER THE NUMBER OF CATEGORIES IN SET 2? 4
ENTER THE FREQUENCY IN SET  1 CATEGORY 1 ? 17
ENTER THE FREQUENCY IN SET  1 CATEGORY 2 ? 6
ENTER THE FREQUENCY IN SET  1 CATEGORY 3 ? 5
ENTER THE FREQUENCY IN SET  2 CATEGORY 1 ? 8
ENTER THE FREQUENCY IN SET  2 CATEGORY 2 ? 13
ENTER THE FREQUENCY IN SET  2 CATEGORY 3 ? 10
ENTER THE FREQUENCY IN SET  3 CATEGORY 1 ? 10
ENTER THE FREQUENCY IN SET  3 CATEGORY 2 ? 12
ENTER THE FREQUENCY IN SET  3 CATEGORY 3 ? 13
ENTER THE FREQUENCY IN SET  4 CATEGORY 1 ? 8
ENTER THE FREQUENCY IN SET  4 CATEGORY 2 ? 9
ENTER THE FREQUENCY IN SET  4 CATEGORY 3 ? 14
```

```
                    SET 1
                        1          2          3       TOTAL (O/E)
SET 2
        1 O             17         6          5          28
        1 E             9.632      8.96       9.408      28

        2 O             8          13         10         31
        2 E             10.664     9.92       10.416     31

        3 O             10         12         13         35
        3 E             12.04      11.2       11.76      35

        4 O             8          9          14         31
        4 E             10.664     9.92       10.416     31

        TOTAL (O/E)     43         40         42         125


                              O:  OBSERVED  FREQUENCY
                              E:  EXPECTED  FREQUENCY
CHI-SQUARE= 12.835295
C= .30515656
 6 DEGREE(S) OF FREEDOM
H(0):0.05>P>0.01
```

The contingency coefficient of 0.31 is significant beyond the 0.05 level enabling the null hypothesis to be rejected at this level in favour of H_1 .(Note that according to Siegel this significance level may be halved to 0.025 for a one-sided test since the data in Table 2 clearly show that H_1 correctly predicts that more highly qualified teachers in F.E. teach maths to higher levels).

Fisher Exact Test for Independent Samples

χ^2 tests are not suitable where any expected cell frequency is 0 or more than 20% of cells have expected frequencies of less than 5. Where this is the case, the Fisher Exact test may be used.

In the 2 sample, 2 category case, the rationale of the test is to calculate the exact probability of the observed frequencies and then to add that of observations more extreme, keeping the same row and column totals in the resulting 2 x 2 contingency table, which is shown in form below and with specific data in the example print-out of the output discussed shortly:

	sample 1	sample 2	TOTAL
category 1	A	B	A+B
category 2	C	D	C+D
TOTAL	A+C	B+D	N=A+B+C+D

Table 3: arrangement of frequency data in the Fisher Exact test 2 x 2 Contingency Table

The exact probability of the observed frequencies A, B, C and D is given by:

$$p = \frac{(A+B)!(C+D)!(A+C)!(B+D)!}{N!A!B!C!D!}$$

The test is one-sided.

A print out of the program is shown on p. 140.

Example

Trigger administered a test of fraction concepts to two groups of hearing-impaired subjects. The experimental group worked through a fractions teaching program before re-taking the test. The control group did not work through the teaching program but simply re-took the test. The frequencies of subjects in each group which improved their test scores on re-testing are shown in Table 4:

	E	C	TOTAL
improvers	4	1	5
non-improvers	3	6	9
TOTAL	7	7	14

Table 4: Table of frequencies of subjects who improved/did not improve their scores after working (E group)/not working(Control group) through a fractions teaching program: E=Experimental Group, C=Control Group

The null hypothesis was that the proportions of subjects who improved/did not improve their test scores after taking/not taking a fractions teaching program are equal. The alternative hypothesis was that a higher proportion of those who took the test showed improvement in their test score.

The E group constitutes sample 1, the C group sample 2.

Note that the small numbers of subjects involved would give rise to expected cell frequencies preventing the two-sample χ^2 test from being used.

A print-out of the output of the program using the above data as input is shown below:

```
run_debug_basic_programs
c:\users\pejt4\Basic_programs>FISHEXACT.BAS
ENTER THE FREQUENCY IN CATEGORY 1 SAMPLE 1 ? 4
ENTER THE FREQUENCY IN CATEGORY 1 SAMPLE 2 ? 1
ENTER THE FREQUENCY IN CATEGORY 2 SAMPLE 1 ? 3
ENTER THE FREQUENCY IN CATEGORY 2 SAMPLE 2 ? 6
THE CONTINGENCY TABLE IS:


SAMPLE 1        SAMPLE 2        TOTAL

CATEGORY 1      4               1               5
CATEGORY 2      3               6               9

TOTAL           7               7               14


P= .13286714
```

Since p>0.05, the null hypothesis could not be rejected at the 5% level of significance. The improvement shown by those taking the test did not exceed chance level.

McNemar Test for Related Samples

The McNemar test is a test for the significance of *changes,* where the data may be laid out in a 2 x2 contingency table as below:

		AFTER	
		decreased	**increased**
	increased	A	B
BEFORE			
	decreased	C	D

Only cells A and D contain information about changes, and so rearranging the χ^2 formula for the 2-sample case quoted earlier with a continuity correction (since a discrete distribution is being approximated by the continuous χ^2 distribution) gives:

$$\chi^2 = \frac{(|A - B| - 1)^2}{A + B}$$

This expression is evaluated on line 320 of the program on p. 142, most of which is concerned with printing out the contingency table and looking up the significance of the calculated χ^2 from the DATA lines at the beginning of the program.

Example

Suppose a group of adults was asked whether they were for or against the development of wind powered electricity generation before and after reading a book making a case against wind power, and that the results below were obtained:

	AFTER reading	
	In Favour	Against
BEFORE reading — In Favour	23	7
Against	13	17

Table 5: frequencies of adults who changed/did not change their attitudes to wind power from 'for' to 'against' or *vice-versa* after reading a book making a case against wind power (artificial data)

The null hypothesis is that the probability that any adult who changes his/her attitude to wind power from for to against after reading the book is equal to the probability that he/she will change his/her attitude to wind power from against to for after reading the book. The alternative hypothesis is that adults show a significant negative attitude change to wind power after reading the book.

A print out of the programs output for this example is shown below:

```
run_debug_basic_programs
Microsoft Windows [Version 6.0.6001]
Copyright (c) 2006 Microsoft Corporation. All rights reserved.

c:\users\pejt4\Basic_programs>mcnemar.bas
MAY BE USED WHERE SUBJECTS ACT AS THEIR OWN CONTROLS . e.g. FREQUENCY OF SUBJECTS
  FAILING A TEST BEFORE TUITION WHO PASS  AFTER TUITION


                          AFTER
                  CATEGORY X          CATEGORY Y
            X     A                   CATEGORY B
BEFORE
            Y     C                   D


ENTER FREQUENCY A? 23
ENTER FREQUENCY B? 7
ENTER FREQUENCY C? 13
ENTER FREQUENCY D? 17
CHI-SQUARE= .625 1 DF

H(O):P>0.1

c:\users\pejt4\Basic_programs>_
```

Since the probability under the null hypothesis associated with the observed value of $\chi^2 = 0.625$ with 1 degree of freedom is greater than 0.1, the null hypothesis cannot be rejected. Adults are no more likely to change their attitudes to wind power from for to against than from against to for after reading the book making a case against wind power.

k- samples

Chi-Square test

We have seen that the χ^2 test may be used for one and two independent samples of nominal data. Calculation of the Continuity coefficient in the test of association required an extension of the *BASIC* program for the 2-sample case to allow for data in more than 2 categories for both characteristics. This involved renaming 'samples' 'set 1' of k categories.

The same program may be simply adapted as a test of differences between frequencies in more than two groups, by changing 'set 1' to samples and omitting the contingency coefficient. A print out of the program is on p. 143-5.

Example

Responses to the YouGov/Sunday Times poll question referred to earlier obtained the following results (frequencies) by "voting intention":

	Con	Lab	Lib. Dem.
Nuclear power	187	112	30
Wind power	74	131	43
Wave/tidal power	79	79	34

The null hypothesis is that the proportion of GB adults mostly supporting the three types of power generation do not differ by voting intention. The alternative hypothesis is that this proportion differs.

The output of the program given the above data is shown below:

```
run_debug_basic_programs - chisq.bas
c:\users\pejt4\Basic_programs>chisq.bas
ENTER THE NUMBER OF SAMPLES ? 3
ENTER THE NUMBER OF CATEGORIES? 3
ENTER THE FREQUENCY IN CATEGORY 1 SAMPLE 1 ? 187
ENTER THE FREQUENCY IN CATEGORY 1 SAMPLE 2 ? 112
ENTER THE FREQUENCY IN CATEGORY 1 SAMPLE 3 ? 30
ENTER THE FREQUENCY IN CATEGORY 2 SAMPLE 1 ? 74
ENTER THE FREQUENCY IN CATEGORY 2 SAMPLE 2 ? 131
ENTER THE FREQUENCY IN CATEGORY 2 SAMPLE 3 ? 43
ENTER THE FREQUENCY IN CATEGORY 3 SAMPLE 1 ? 79
ENTER THE FREQUENCY IN CATEGORY 3 SAMPLE 2 ? 79
ENTER THE FREQUENCY IN CATEGORY 3 SAMPLE 3 ? 34_

                 SAMPLE
                    1           2          3        TOTAL (O/E)
CATEGORY
     1 O          187         112         30          329
     1 E      145.46164  137.76073  45.777634      329

     2 O           74         131         43          248
     2 E      109.648895 103.843956 34.507153      248

     3 O           79          79         34          192
     3 E      84.889465   80.39532  26.715214      192

        TOTAL (O/E)   340         322        107         769

                        O: OBSERVED FREQUENCY
                        E:  EXPECTED FREQUENCY
CHI-SQUARE= 45.317986
H(0):P<0.01
```

Since the probability under H_0 of obtaining a χ^2 value as high as that obtained is less than 0.01, the decision is to reject H_0 in favour of H_1 that the proportion of GB adults mostly supporting the three types of power generation differ by voting intention.

Lastly in this chapter we come to consider a test for related k-sample nominal data.

Cochran Q Test

This is an extension of the McNemar test for two related samples discussed earlier to more than two related samples. The aim of the test is to determine whether the frequencies for each sample differ in one or more characteristics. The dichotomous data (pass/fail, 0/1, yes/no, etc.) may be in the form of repeated measures on the same individuals, or samples may be of different individuals matched on relevant attributes. If there are N samples and k characteristics, a formula for Q, which may be tested against the value of χ^2 with k-1 degrees of freedom under the null hypothesis, is:

$$Q = \frac{(k-1) \left[k \sum_{j-1}^{k} G_j^2 - \left(\sum_{j=1}^{k} G_j \right)^2 \right]}{k \sum_{i=1}^{N} L_i - \sum_{i-1}^{N} L_i^2}$$

where G_j is the total number of passes/1's/yeses, etc. in the jth sample; L_i is the total number 1's/yeses, etc. for each characteristic.

A print out of the program is on pp. 146- 7.

Example

Previously in the discussion of different types of sample in Chapter 1, the scenario of 3 related samples of subjects who rated aesthetically three types of tower construction supporting a wind turbine- lattice, concrete 'telescopic' and steel tubular (the 'characteristics') was described. We will imagine that each group consists of 8 individuals suitably matched on relevant attributes. For instance, each subject might be asked to rate a photograph of an example of one of the three type of tower construction, selected at random. This is a matched subjects design with 3 characteristics. For entry into the program, Characteristic 1 will denote the lattice tower type, Characteristic 2 the concrete telescopic type of tower and Characteristic 3 the steel tubular type.

'1' will be entered for a type of tower construction, which a subject likes, '0' for a 'disliked' one.

Suppose the results of the study were as follows:

	subject	tower (charact -eristic)	lattice (1)	concrete (2)	tubular (3)
sample1	1		1		
	2			0	
	3				1
sample2	1		0		
	2			0	
	3				1
sample3	1		0		
	2			0	
	3				1
sample4	1		1		
	2			0	
	3				1
sample5	1		1		
	2			0	
	3				1
sample6	1		1		
	2			0	
	3				0
sample7	1		0		
	2			0	
	3				0

52

tower (charact-eristic)	lattice (1)	concrete (2)	tubular (3)
sample8 1	0		
2		0	
3			1

Table 6: subjects like/dislike of 3 types of tower

Note that if a repeated measures design had been used with 8 subjects, each rating all 3 towers, and the frequencies in Table 7 had been obtained, the value of Q would be the same.

A print out of the input to output from the program for this example is shown below:

```
run_debug_basic_programs - cochranq.bas
Microsoft Windows [Version 6.0.6001]
Copyright (c) 2006 Microsoft Corporation.  All rights reserved.

c:\users\pejt4\Basic_programs>cochranq.bas
COCHRAN Q TEST FOR N RELATED SAMPLES OF DICHOTMOUS DATA
(pass/fail; 0/1; yes/no, etc.)
Each subject may be rated once on one characteristic in a matched subjects design
or a given subject may be rated on each characteristic in a repeated measures design
REPEATED MEASURES DESIGN PRESS [r]; MATCHED SUBJECTS DESIGN PRESS [m]? m
HOW MANY CHRACTERISTICS? 3
HOW MANY SAMPLES? 8
ENTER [0] FOR FAIL/NO/ZERO, ETC. OR [1] FOR PASS/YES/ONE,ETC FOR SUBJECT  1
SAMPLE 1 CHARACTERISTIC 1 ? 1
ENTER [0] FOR FAIL/NO/ZERO, ETC. OR [1] FOR PASS/YES/ONE,ETC FOR SUBJECT  2
SAMPLE 1 CHARACTERISTIC 2 ? 0
ENTER [0] FOR FAIL/NO/ZERO, ETC. OR [1] FOR PASS/YES/ONE,ETC FOR SUBJECT  3
SAMPLE 1 CHARACTERISTIC 3 ? 1
ENTER [0] FOR FAIL/NO/ZERO, ETC. OR [1] FOR PASS/YES/ONE,ETC FOR SUBJECT  1
SAMPLE 2 CHARACTERISTIC 1 ? 0
ENTER [0] FOR FAIL/NO/ZERO, ETC. OR [1] FOR PASS/YES/ONE,ETC FOR SUBJECT  2
SAMPLE 2 CHARACTERISTIC 2 ? 0
ENTER [0] FOR FAIL/NO/ZERO, ETC. OR [1] FOR PASS/YES/ONE,ETC FOR SUBJECT  3
SAMPLE 2 CHARACTERISTIC 3 ? 1
ENTER [0] FOR FAIL/NO/ZERO, ETC. OR [1] FOR PASS/YES/ONE,ETC FOR SUBJECT  1
SAMPLE 3 CHARACTERISTIC 1 ? 0
ENTER [0] FOR FAIL/NO/ZERO, ETC. OR [1] FOR PASS/YES/ONE,ETC FOR SUBJECT  2
SAMPLE 3 CHARACTERISTIC 2 ? 0
ENTER [0] FOR FAIL/NO/ZERO, ETC. OR [1] FOR PASS/YES/ONE,ETC FOR SUBJECT  3
SAMPLE 3 CHARACTERISTIC 3 ? 1
ENTER [0] FOR FAIL/NO/ZERO, ETC. OR [1] FOR PASS/YES/ONE,ETC FOR SUBJECT  1
SAMPLE 4 CHARACTERISTIC 1 ? 1
ENTER [0] FOR FAIL/NO/ZERO, ETC. OR [1] FOR PASS/YES/ONE,ETC FOR SUBJECT  2
SAMPLE 4 CHARACTERISTIC 2 ? 0
ENTER [0] FOR FAIL/NO/ZERO, ETC. OR [1] FOR PASS/YES/ONE,ETC FOR SUBJECT  3
SAMPLE 4 CHARACTERISTIC 3 ? 1
```

```
ENTER [0] FOR FAIL/NO/ZERO, ETC. OR [1] FOR PASS/YES/ONE,ETC FOR SUBJECT 1
SAMPLE 5 CHARACTERISTIC 1 ? 1
ENTER [0] FOR FAIL/NO/ZERO, ETC. OR [1] FOR PASS/YES/ONE,ETC FOR SUBJECT 2
SAMPLE 5 CHARACTERISTIC 2 ? 0
ENTER [0] FOR FAIL/NO/ZERO, ETC. OR [1] FOR PASS/YES/ONE,ETC FOR SUBJECT 3
SAMPLE 5 CHARACTERISTIC 3 ? 1
ENTER [0] FOR FAIL/NO/ZERO, ETC. OR [1] FOR PASS/YES/ONE,ETC FOR SUBJECT 1
SAMPLE 6 CHARACTERISTIC 1 ? 1
ENTER [0] FOR FAIL/NO/ZERO, ETC. OR [1] FOR PASS/YES/ONE,ETC FOR SUBJECT 2
SAMPLE 6 CHARACTERISTIC 2 ? 0
ENTER [0] FOR FAIL/NO/ZERO, ETC. OR [1] FOR PASS/YES/ONE,ETC FOR SUBJECT 3
SAMPLE 6 CHARACTERISTIC 3 ? 0
ENTER [0] FOR FAIL/NO/ZERO, ETC. OR [1] FOR PASS/YES/ONE,ETC FOR SUBJECT 1
SAMPLE 7 CHARACTERISTIC 1 ? 0
ENTER [0] FOR FAIL/NO/ZERO, ETC. OR [1] FOR PASS/YES/ONE,ETC FOR SUBJECT 2
SAMPLE 7 CHARACTERISTIC 2 ? 0
ENTER [0] FOR FAIL/NO/ZERO, ETC. OR [1] FOR PASS/YES/ONE,ETC FOR SUBJECT 3
SAMPLE 7 CHARACTERISTIC 3 ? 0
ENTER [0] FOR FAIL/NO/ZERO, ETC. OR [1] FOR PASS/YES/ONE,ETC FOR SUBJECT 1
SAMPLE 8 CHARACTERISTIC 1 ? 0
ENTER [0] FOR FAIL/NO/ZERO, ETC. OR [1] FOR PASS/YES/ONE,ETC FOR SUBJECT 2
SAMPLE 8 CHARACTERISTIC 2 ? 0
ENTER [0] FOR FAIL/NO/ZERO, ETC. OR [1] FOR PASS/YES/ONE,ETC FOR SUBJECT 3
SAMPLE 8 CHARACTERISTIC 3 ? 1

Q= 8  ( 2 DF)

H(0):0.05>P>0.01

c:\users\pejt4\Basic_programs>_
```

A Q of 8 with 2 degrees of freedom has a probability of between 0.05 and 0.01, and so the null hypothesis can be rejected at the 0.05 level of significance in favour of H_1 . The frequencies obtained indicate that the tubular tower was liked the most, followed by the steel lattice type. The telescopic concrete tower was not liked at all.

In Chapter 4, we move on to consider the computerisation of tests for data which are in at least an ordinal scale.

4. PROGRAMMING TESTS FOR ORDINAL DATA

One sample

<u>The Kolmogorov-Smirnov One Sample Test</u>

This is a 'goodness of fit test' which compares the distribution of the data with a distribution chosen by the user. This latter is input to the program in the form of cumulative proportions for each datum, i.e., the proportion of values in the chosen distribution which are equal to or less than the value of that datum. The test then determines the maximum deviation D, known as the 'Kolmogorov distance' between this proportion and the corresponding proportion obtained. Values of D corresponding to various significance levels for a given sample size under the null hypothesis of no difference are available from tables, from which the goodness of fit of the data to the chosen distribution can be determined.

The DATA statements at the beginning of the computer program shown on pp. 148-149 contain the critical values of D for each of 5 significance levels from Table E in Spiegel. These are read into the array critd(i,j). Next, the observed data are inputted by the user, which the program ranks in ascending order. The user is then asked to enter the cumulative probabilities of each datum value calculated from his/her chosen distribution. An example will be given below for the NORMAL distribution, but any distribution might be chosen.

The program then prints out the ranked data, the observed cumulative probabilities and the user entered probabilities from the chosen distribution to which the goodness of fit of the data is being tested. If there are more than 1 screenful of data, the program will pause until the user presses a key to print out the remaining values, but the user should first note down the maximum deviation. After all the data and chosen distribution cumulative probabilities have been printed out, the user is asked to determine the maximum deviance between any data distribution cumulative probability the chosen distribution cumulative probability pair. The program looks up this value in the table of critical deviations and comes up with the associated probability under H_0 of obtaining a value this large.

An example will make the foregoing clear.

Example

Trigger (1985) administered a test of fraction

concepts to 30 individuals and tested the scores obtained for goodness of fit to a normal distribution using the Kolomogorov-Smirnov one sample test.

She had first to calculate the cumulative probabilities associated with each datum value under the null hypothesis that they came from a NORMAL distribution. (This process could be avoided by adapting the program specifically for testing the goodness of fit to a NORMAL distribution- which would, of course, make the program much less versatile- by reading in cumulative probabilities of standardized normal values from tables, calculating the z values of the data, and looking up the associated tabulated value, from which the deviances could be determined. However, typing in the large amount of data required is tedious and error-prone).

To do this, the mean and sample standard deviation for each of the data were calculated, and their associated z values determined using the relationship:

z = (datum value-mean)/standard deviation. The cumulative probability of the datum under H_0 was then looked up in tables.

The table below shows the scores obtained from

testing and their normal cumulative probabilities:

datum number	test score	cumulative probability under H_0
1	8	.1284
2	11	.64314
3	9	.26314
4	11	.64314
5	11	.64314
6	12	.80707
7	6	.0164
8	11	.64314
9	12	.80707
10	12	.80707
11	6	.0164
12	12	.80707
13	12	.80707
14	9	.26314
15	12	.26314
16	8	.1284
17	8	.1284
18	9	.26314
19	11	.64314
20	12	.80707

datum number	test score	cumulative probability under H_0
21	10	.44693
22	7	.0511
23	12	.80707
24	12	.80707
25	9	.26314
26	12	.80707
27	12	.80707
28	12	.80707
29	8	.1284
30	12	.80707

Table 7: Cumulative probabilities of the scores of 30 individuals on a fractions concept test

Entering these values into the program gave the following input/output:

```
[c] run_debug_basic_programs - kolmog1s.bas
Microsoft Windows [Version 6.0.6001]
Copyright (c) 2006 Microsoft Corporation.  All rights reserved.

c:\users\pejt4\Basic_programs>kolmog1s.bas
Kolmogorov-Smirnov One Sample Test of Goodness of Fit to a user- chosen distribution
DATA CAN BE RAW VALUES OR RANKS
HOW MANY DATA? 30
ENTER DATUM 1 ? 8
ENTER DATUM 2 ? 11
ENTER DATUM 3 ? 9
ENTER DATUM 4 ? 11
ENTER DATUM 5 ? 11
ENTER DATUM 6 ? 12
ENTER DATUM 7 ? 6
ENTER DATUM 8 ? 11
ENTER DATUM 9 ? 12
ENTER DATUM 10 ? 12
ENTER DATUM 11 ? 6
ENTER DATUM 12 ? 12
ENTER DATUM 13 ? 12
ENTER DATUM 14 ? 9
ENTER DATUM 15 ? 12
ENTER DATUM 16 ? 8
ENTER DATUM 17 ? 8
ENTER DATUM 18 ? 9
ENTER DATUM 19 ? 11
ENTER DATUM 20 ? 12
ENTER DATUM 21 ? 10
ENTER DATUM 22 ? 7
ENTER DATUM 23 ? 12
ENTER DATUM 24 ? 12
ENTER DATUM 25 ? 9
ENTER DATUM 26 ? 12
ENTER DATUM 27 ? 12
ENTER DATUM 28 ? 12
ENTER DATUM 29 ? 8
ENTER DATUM 30 ? 12
```

DATUM	OBSERVED CUMULATIVE p	CUMULATIVE P UNDER Ho
6	3.3333335E-2	.0164
6	.06666667	.0164
7	.1	.0511
8	.13333334	.1284
8	.16666667	.1284
8	.2	.1284
8	.23333333	.1284
9	.26666668	.26314
9	.3	.26314
9	.33333334	.26314
9	.36666667	.26314
10	.4	.44693
11	.43333334	.64314
11	.46666667	.64314
11	.5	.64314
11	.53333336	.64314
11	.56666666	.64314
12	.6	.80707
12	.6333333	.80707
12	.6666667	.80707
12	.7	.80707
12	.73333335	.80707
12	.76666665	.80707
12	.8	.80707
12	.8333333	.80707
12	.8666667	.80707
12	.9	.80707
12	.93333334	.80707
12	.96666664	.80707

MORE (NOTE DOWN MAX. DEVIATION SO FAR BEFORE PRESSING ANY KEY?

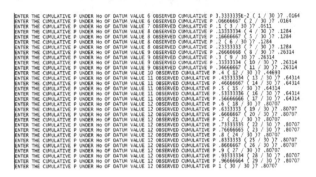

```
ENTER MAX. DEVIANCE BY INSPECTION OF ABOVE TABLE? .20980666

2-SIDED P= .12548335
c:\users\pejt4\Basic_programs>
```

The entries are very repetitive in this example because of the large number of ties in the data. Since the probability of the obtained value of D under H_0 is greater than 0.05, the decision is to accept the null hypothesis that the test scores are drawn from a normal distribution.

One sample Runs Test

The one sample runs test is a test of whether the data in a sample are random in the order in which they occur. The data are first dichomotized according to some criterion, and then each datum is appropriately assigned a 0 or 1. Each consecutive datum is examined in turn, and compared with the previous datum. If it is the same, that and the previous datum constitute part of the same 'run'. If it is different, it starts a new run. For example:

000 11 0 1111 00 1

contains 6 runs, 3 of 0's and 3 of 1's. The total number of runs, and the number of runs in each category, depending on sample size, is used to determine whether or not the sample is random from look-up tables. If N>20, a normal approximation is used and the program returns the associated z value, from which the user may determine the associated significance level from tables.

Example

Suppose we are interested in confirming or disconfirming that the data in Table 6 are randomly ordered. Entering them into the program gives the output:

```
run_debug_basic_programs
Microsoft Windows [Version 6.0.6001]
Copyright (c) 2006 Microsoft Corporation.  All rights reserved.

c:\users\pejt4\Basic_programs>runstest1s.bas
ENTER THE NUMBER OF DATA? 24
ENTER 1 OR 0 FOR DATUM 1 ? 1
ENTER 1 OR 0 FOR DATUM 2 ? 0
ENTER 1 OR 0 FOR DATUM 3 ? 1
ENTER 1 OR 0 FOR DATUM 4 ? 0
ENTER 1 OR 0 FOR DATUM 5 ? 0
ENTER 1 OR 0 FOR DATUM 6 ? 1
ENTER 1 OR 0 FOR DATUM 7 ? 0
ENTER 1 OR 0 FOR DATUM 8 ? 0
ENTER 1 OR 0 FOR DATUM 9 ? 1
ENTER 1 OR 0 FOR DATUM 10 ? 1
ENTER 1 OR 0 FOR DATUM 11 ? 0
ENTER 1 OR 0 FOR DATUM 12 ? 1
ENTER 1 OR 0 FOR DATUM 13 ? 1
ENTER 1 OR 0 FOR DATUM 14 ? 0
ENTER 1 OR 0 FOR DATUM 15 ? 1
ENTER 1 OR 0 FOR DATUM 16 ? 1
ENTER 1 OR 0 FOR DATUM 17 ? 0
ENTER 1 OR 0 FOR DATUM 18 ? 0
ENTER 1 OR 0 FOR DATUM 19 ? 0
ENTER 1 OR 0 FOR DATUM 20 ? 0
ENTER 1 OR 0 FOR DATUM 21 ? 0
ENTER 1 OR 0 FOR DATUM 22 ? 0
ENTER 1 OR 0 FOR DATUM 23 ? 0
ENTER 1 OR 0 FOR DATUM 24 ? 1


R= 13    N1= 10    N2= 14
P>0.05. ORDERING OF DATA IS RANDOM
```

confirming the null hypothesis..

Two samples

Spearman Correlation Test

The Spearman correlation test is a test of association between two samples of data which may be assigned ranks. The Spearman rank correlation coefficient quantifies the degree of this association and is determined by entering the ranked data for each sample into the formula:

$$R_S = \frac{\sum X.Y}{\sqrt{\sum x^2 \sum y^2}}$$

a simplified form of which is:

$$R_S = 1 - \frac{6 \sum_{i=1}^{N} d_i^2}{N^3 - N}$$

This formula is used in the program in line 940 as shown in the print out on pp. 152-4.

In testing R_S for significance, the formula

$$t = R_S \sqrt{\frac{N - 2}{1 - R_S^2}}$$

is in line 2090 and the associated critical values of t for various significance levels for N>30 are in the DATA lines at the start of the program. The DATA statements following contain a look-up table for critical values of R_S for N<=30. The next part of the program ranks the two samples of data, calculates R_S and looks up the corresponding significance value. The output value of R_S is uncorrected for ties, but if there are many ties, a corrected value may be obtained by entering:

$$Tx = \sum_X \frac{t^3 - t}{12}$$

and

$$Ty = \sum_Y \frac{t^3 - t}{12}$$

where t is the number of tied data in a group with

the same rank, and Tx and Ty are summed over all groups of ties in sample x and sample y respectively. The forthcoming example will make this clear. Alternatively, the first formula on p. 63 may be used, after obtaining the ranked data for the two samples which is printed out by the program.

The power of the test, compared with the Pearson correlation parametric test equivalent, is 91%.

Example

Teachers of the 30 individuals involved in fraction concepts testing described on pp. 55-8 above were asked to rate their understanding of fraction concepts on a scale of 1-4. The results obtained are in the following table:

Test score	Teacher's Rating
8	3
11	4
9	4
11	4
11	4
12	4
6	2
11	3

Test score	Teacher's Rating
12	4
12	4
6	2
12	4
12	4
9	3
12	4
8	3
8	2
9	3
9	3
11	3
12	4
10	4
7	2
12	4
12	4
9	3
12	4
12	4
12	4
8	2

Table 8: Teachers' Ratings of 30 testees' fraction concepts

When entered into the program, the following output was obtained:

```
run_debug_basic_programs
 SPEARMAN Rs (UNCOORECTED FOR TIES)= .87931037
CORRECTION FOR TIES:
USE PEARSON CORRELATION OR
ENTER SIGMA Tx? 210
ENTER SIGMA Ty? 372.5
SPEARMAN Rs (CORRECTED FOR TIES) .8620857
P<0.01
```

The null hypothesis of no association between fraction concepts test score and teachers' ratings is rejected beyond the 0.01 level of significance in favour of the alternative (one-sided) hypothesis that fraction concept test scores and teachers' ratings are positively related (since Rs is positive: if Rs had been negative, it would have implied that high fraction test scores are associated with low teacher ratings).

Median Test for Two Independent Samples

The median test tests the likelihood that two samples were taken from populations with the same median (the null hypothesis). The alternative hypothesis may be one- or two sided (that Sample 1 or 2 median > Sample 2 or 1 median (specifying which). After the user enters the data in each sample, the data are ranked as a whole, the grand median calculated, and then ranks are assigned to each datum in each sample. The program then produces a 2 x 2 contingency table whose entries are the frequency of data above/below the grand median in samples 1/2. A chi-square 2-sample test may then be applied to the entries in the table, or the Fisher Exact test if the sample sizes are small.

The median test program print-out is shown on pp. 155-6.

Example

A question in the questionnaire survey in Trigger (1985) obtained information from two groups of teachers about the articles or books they had read in in connection with their professional interests. The raw data are reproduced below:

Teacher group 1 *Numbers of books/articles*

2 3 1 2 3 4 5 3 2 2

5 1 2 2 3 1 2 3 1 2

2 2

Teacher group 2 5 6 4 5 7 3 6 8 5 5

4 6 6 5 4 7 5

Table 9: Professional Reading interests of Two samples of teachers

The null hypothesis was of no difference in the median number of articles or books read in the populations from which the teachers were drawn. H_1 was that the medians are different.

Entering this data in the program produced the following output:

```
run_debug_basic_programs
THE RANKED DATA FOR THE SAMPLES COMBINED IS:
 1  1  1  1  2  2  2  2  2  2  2  2  2  2

 3  3  3  3  3  3  4  4  4  4  5  5  5  5

 5  5  5  5  6  6  6  6  7  7  8



MEDIAN= 3

                      SAMPLE 1           SAMPLE 2
ABOVE G/MEDIAN           8                 17
BELOW G/MEDIAN          14                  0
CHI-SQUARE= 14.224199  (1 DEGREE OF FREEDOM)

H(0):P<0.01
```

H_0 can be rejected at the 0.01 significance level in favour of H_1. It appears from the questionnaire data that teachers in the second group read more articles or books in connection with their professional interests.

Mann-Whitney 'U' Test

The data in the above example, used for the purposes of illustration of the method, are better suited to tests for ranked data, such as the Mann-Whitney 'U' test which makes use of the additional information available in ranked data, and which therefore evinces greater power than the Median test. In fact, when compared with the 't' test on data suitable for parametric tests, the Mann-Whitney test has a power approaching 95%, compared with that of 63% of the Median test.

The Mann-Whitney test tests the null hypothesis that two samples are from populations with same distribution. The complete data set is first ranked, and the ranks are assigned to one of the samples from lowest to highest. The value 'U' is the number of times each datum in that sample is less than a datum in the other sample, with any negative values being considered as less than 0 or positive values. The probability that a given value of U will be as extreme as that obtained from the data under the null hypothesis is given in tables. However, in this case the normal approximation is good provided there are not too many ties and the numbers of data in each sample are 8 or more (Daly et al. (1995)). The program therefore provides significance values for samples of 8 or more, but tables of U values covering every contingency for sample sizes up to 7 are extensive, and so for smaller samples, a 'U' value only is given with which the reader may refer to tables of critical U values such as in Siegel itself or Neave or an electronic/www. source.

In using the normal approximation, the mean is taken to be n.m/2, where n and m are the sample sizes, with variance m.n.(m+n+1)/12, the resulting associated standard normal z value is therefore:

$$z = \frac{U - m.n/2}{\sqrt{m.n.(m+n+1)/12}}$$

The program for the test is shown on pp. 157-8. Note that this program is exceptional in that the original *BASIC* had to be modified slightly at line 545 to run in *Vintbas*, which has no MIN (parameter1,parameter2) instruction. No correction is made for ties, which is comparatively small, but would tend to increase the value of Z slightly.

Example

Another question in the questionnaire survey in Trigger (1985) asked respondents in the two groups of teachers how many hours of timetabled teaching time they spent teaching mathematics. The results are tabulated below:

Teacher group 1	*No. of hours teaching maths*									
	9	7	6	12	8	9	10	8	14	11
	8	8	8	7	6	5	8	9	10	9
	6	-								

Teacher group 2	22	17	23	18	20	16	15
	20	14	24	18	19	25	21	17
	19	20					

Table 10: The number of hours of time-tabled teaching time spent teaching mathematics by two groups of teachers.

The null hypothesis was that the teaching times come from populations with the same distribution.

The test performed in the program is two-sided, and so for directional hypotheses the quoted probability should be halved. The output of the program for this data is shown below:

```
run_debug_basic_programs

U= .5
Z=-5.225697
P<0.01

c:\users\pejt4\Basic_programs>_
```

H_0 may be rejected beyond the 0.01 level of significance, the higher values associated with the second group of teachers being quite obvious.

Sign Test for 2 Related Samples

When the data are in pairs from samples matched in relevant characteristics or represent 'repeated measures' on the same individuals, and the data in each pair can be ranked with respect to each other, i.e., in a pair of data AB, datum A>datum B, datum B>datum A or datum A=datum B, the sign test may be applied. The rationale of the test is that, under the null hypothesis one datum in each pair is no more likely to be greater than the other. H_0 may therefore be tested by counting the number of pairs of data evincing a 'greater than' or 'less than' relationship (which ever is the least), and using the binomial formula:

$$^{n}C_{x} = \sum_{n=1}^{x} \frac{N!}{x!(N-x)!}$$

The program, whose print-out is shown on p. 159, incorporates a normal approximation for sample sizes >=25.

Example

Trigger (*op. cit.*), tested the fraction concepts of 20 subjects on one whole shape followed by another, obtaining the overall percentage correct in each case. The null hypothesis was of an equal likelihood that scores for one shape would be greater than for two shapes as that scores for two shapes would be greater than for one shape. A 2-sided alternative was chosen. The data input to the program is tabulated below:

	one shape	two shapes
Percentage score	50	62.5
	75	70
	25	37.5
	100	100
	100	100
	25	50
	75	87.5
	50	50
	75	75
	100	100
	75	70
	75	87.5
	75	87.5
	25	37.5
	75	75
	50	62.5
	100	100
	100	100
	100	100
	50	62.5

Table 11: percentage scores of 20 subjects in a fractions test with one and two whole shapes

The output of the program is shown below:

```
run_debug_basic_programs
(SAMPLE1-SAMPLE2)+  OBSERVED (EXPECTED)(SAMPLE1-SAMPLE2)-  OBSERVED (EXPECTED)
 2 ( 5.5 )                        9 ( 5.5 )
P= 5.859375E-3
```

The column headed '+' relates to the number of pairs of data in which the sample 1 datum >

sample 2 datum; vice versa in the '-' column. There were 9 ties. The one-sided probability is 0.006, giving a 2-sided probability (since the binomial distribution is symmetrical for p=0.5) of 0.012, and the null hypothesis can be rejected at this level in favour of the alternative hypothesis.

Wilcoxon 2 sample Signed-Ranks test

The second test for two related samples with ordinal data makes use of information in the data where each datum in each pair may be ranked in relation to its partner, *and* where each pair may be ranked with respect to every other pair. Not only does the sign test ignore the latter, but it ignores data pairs in which one datum is neither greater nor less than the other (i.e. they are equal in value) . Consequently, whereas the power of the sign test approaches only 63% relative to the 't' test, the

Wilcoxon test manages 95%, and so the Wilcoxon test should be used in preference to the Sign test where the data may be ranked between as well as within sample 1- sample 2 matched pairs. The effect of this will be seen when we compare the results of the Wilcoxon analysis with the Sign test analysis in the example previously used with the sign test. A print out of the program is on pp. 160-1.

Example

Suppose we re-analyze the data in the last example using the Wilcoxon test. The output from program is:

```
c:\ run_debug_basic_programs

DIFFERENCE                              RANK
 5                                       1.5
 5                                       1.5
-12.5                                    6.5
-12.5                                    6.5
-12.5                                    6.5
-12.5                                    6.5
-12.5                                    6.5
-12.5                                    6.5
-12.5                                    6.5
-25                                     11


T= 3
N= 11
2-SIDED:
p<0.01

c:\users\pejt4\Basic_programs>
```

The 2-sided probability that scores are no different for two whole shapes than one is now <0.01 whereas the sign test returned a 2 sided probability of >0.01, indicating the superior power of the Wilcoxon test over the sign test.

80

k samples

Kendall Concordance Test

Kendall's Concordance test can be used as a test of association between more than two samples on several characteristics, where the characteristics comprise ranked data. The Kendall Concordance coefficient, W, is a measure of how different the observed rankings in the k samples are from equality.

To calculate W, the data for each of N characteristics is ranked across the k samples. The deviation of the of the sum of ranks for each characteristic from the mean sum of ranks for the N characteristics combined, s, is then determined, where

$$s = \sum_{\text{all characteristics}} (\text{sum of ranks for characteristic} - \text{sum of ranks for all characteristics} /N)^2$$

the sum of squares of the deviations from the mean.

The maximum sum of squares of deviations occurs when the rankings across the k groups and N characteristics are equal, and this is equal to:

$$S = \frac{1}{12} k^2 (N^3 - N)$$

W is therefore given by W=s/S. This is the expression at line 370 in the program print out on pp. 162-4. The Spearman rank correlation coefficients for each pair of samples can be calculated from W and are printed out at line 390. If there are fewer than 8 characteristics, a look up table must be used to determine the significance of W under the null hypothesis. If N>=8, k(N-1).W offers a good approximation to chi-square with N-1 degrees of freedom (see line 410). It is important to incorporate a correction for ties in samples, using the procedure explained on p.64, since when there are many ties, as in the example below, the uncorrected value of W is too low and therefore the value of the significance of W is too high. Siegel, for instance, gives an example where the significance value associated with the test statistic is halved after correcting for ties. Here, this accomplished by lines 330-370.

Example

In the author's Ph.D (Lond) research, she was interested in the relative difficulty of solving problems involving finding 1/2's, 1/3's, 1/4's and 1/10's of whole shapes. She cast the results of testing (scores) as shown in the table below:

fraction test scores		1/2	1/4	1/3	1/10
subject	1	3	3	2	0
	2	3	3	3	2
	3	3	2	1	0
	4	3	2	2	1
	5	3	3	3	2
	6	3	3	1	0
	7	3	3	3	0
	8	3	3	3	2
	9	3	3	3	2
	10	3	3	3	2
	11	3	1	2	0
	12	3	3	3	0
	13	3	3	2	0
	14	3	3	2	0

Table 12: Fraction test scores for four fractions

Here, the 14 subjects are the 'samples', and the 4 fractions the 'characteristics'. With this data, the output of the program obtained is shown below:

```
run_debug_basic_programs
W= .85914546 CORRECTED FOR TIES
AVERAGE SPEARMAN Rs FOR EACH PAIR OF SAMPLES = .8483105
P<0.01

c:\users\pejt4\Basic_programs>_
```

The high values of W obtained enables the null hypothesis that the ranks of scores across the four fractions do not differ to be rejected at the 0.01 level of significance. The data indicate the order of difficulty 1/10>1/3>1/4>1/2 in support of Piagetian theory (Piaget et al. (1960)).

Kruskal-Wallis One-Way Analysis of Variance (ANOVAR) for k independent samples

The Kruskal-Wallis ANOVAR for ranked data tests whether the data in each of k samples could have been drawn from the same population of different populations with the same medians and variances. It does this by ranking the complete data set and then comparing the ranks within each sample. The test statistic is H, where

$$H = \frac{12}{N(N+1)} \sum_{j=1}^{k} \frac{R_j^2}{n_j} - 3(N+1)$$

and k= the number of samples, n_j the number of data in the jth sample and R_j the sum of ranks in the jth sample. A correction for ties is made along the lines previously described, giving rise to the factor

$$1- \frac{\sum_{j=1}^{k} T_j}{N^3 - N}$$

where the T_j are the T_X, T_Y, ... T_K are as described on p. 64. This is a very powerful test, almost as powerful as the parametric F test.

H has a near chi-square distribution where the numbers in each sample are more than 5, with k-1 degrees of freedom. For smaller sample sizes, it will be necessary to consult a reference table of critical values of H, for example in Siegel or Neave. For $n_j > 5$, the program whose print-out is shown on pp. 165-7 outputs the value of H and the associated significance value.

In transferring the program from the Locomotive 1984 *BASIC* on the *Amstrad PCW8256* this time there were two differences between the *BASIC*s which necessitated modifications to the original program. The first was to with the way the *Vintbas BASIC* behaved in executing the TAB instruction if the position of the print head has already passed the position calculated in the next TAB instruction (see line 1020. See also Alcock (1981, p. 33)). Whereas Locomotive *BASIC* in this case executes a carriage return (i.e., starts a new line), *Vintbas BASIC* continues along the same line. Without correction, this resulted in a messed-up print out of the table of sample values x ranks. The solution was to add a PRINT instruction at the ends of lines 1020, 1035 and 1060 to force a carriage return after printing the rank of the last sample in each row (absent in the Locomotive *BASIC* version).

The second difference which resulted in ranks being misplaced in the sample x ranks table and an uncorrected value of H was due to differences in the IF (condition(s)) instruction where there were two conditions (see line 1020). Unnecessary in the Locomotive *BASIC* version, the conditions of the IF statement had to be enclosed in brackets in the *Vintbas* version.

<u>Example</u>

The author used this test to compare the total fraction concept scores of three groups of ten individuals. Their scores are tabulated below:

FRACTION TEST SCORES

		Group1	*Group2*	*Group3*
Subject	1	8	11	9
	2	11	11	12
	3	6	11	12
	4	12	6	12
	5	12	9	12
	6	8	8	10
	7	11	12	11
	8	7	12	12
	9	9	12	12
	10	12	8	12

Table 13: The Fraction Concepts Test scores of 3 samples of individuals (Trigger (1985)).

The output of the program fed with this data is as follows:

```
run_debug_basic_programs

RANKINGS BY SAMPLE


 1          2          3

1.5        5.5        9
9          14.5       24
24         1.5        11
14.5       24         14.5
14.5       24         24
24         5.5        24
24         9          24
3          14.5       24
5.5        14.5       24
5.5        24         24

H= 4.4522476

CORRECTED FOR TIES, H= 4.903909

       DEGREES OF FREEDOM = 2

Ho: 0.1>P>0.05

c:\users\pejt4\Basic_programs>
```

Hence the author concluded that there was weak evidence against the null hypothesis of no difference between the populations from which the samples were drawn, but the null hypothesis can not be rejected at the 0.05 significance level, even though the power of this test is such that an

F-Test on the same data gave a F=2.49 on 2 degrees of freedom with an associated significance value of 0.102, compared with an exact significance value associated with H (corrected for ties) using electronic tables of 0.086 in the *Texas TI-83 Plus*.

Friedman two-way Analysis of Variance for k Related Samples

The Friedman 2-way ANOVAR is applicable to N ranked data on each of k characteristics in k matched samples. The test tests the null hypothesis that the k samples have been drawn from the same population.

This is another very powerful test, which, according to Friedman, is as capable as the corresponding parametric analysis of variance test in rejecting a null hypothesis when it is false (Friedman (1937), cited in Siegel).

The test statistic, χ_r is approximately distributed as χ^2 with k-1 degrees of freedom, and is given by:

$$\chi^2_r = \frac{12}{Nk(k+1)} \sum_{j=1}^{k} (R_j)^2 - 3N(k+1)$$

The expression in the rhs is evaluated at line 332 in a program carrying out the test on pp. 168-69. The program prints out the value of χ^2 and the associated significance under H_0 where the number of samples and the number of data in each sample is 5 or more. For values <5, the user should consult tables of critical values of χ^2 (Such as Siegel, pp. 280-281).

Example

Suppose we are interested in comparing 6 colleges on the mathematics achievement test scores of 5 sets of 6 matched students within each set, with one student in each set attending a different one of the 6 colleges. The matching might be done on the basis of age, intelligence and sex, for example. A table of average scores (percentages) for each set of subjects is shown below:

% (AVERAGE) TEST SCORES   ***College***

		A	B	C	D	E	F
sets of subjects	1	73	65	77	59	67	71
	2	68	72	70	71	58	63
	3	79	75	75	69	68	74
	4	57	62	63	68	67	58
	5	70	59	61	66	72	69

Table 14:   Average scores of 5 sets of matched subjects in 6 colleges on a mathematics achievement test

The output from the program using this data is show below:

```
run_debug_basic_programs

CHISQUARE= 1.4285736 ON    5 DEGREES OF FREEDOM
H(0):P>0.1
c:\users\pejt4\Basic_programs>
```

The very low value of the obtained chi-square on 5 degrees of freedom indicates that there is little difference in the mathematics test achievement scores of pupils across the 6 colleges.

The last of the three chapters dealing with statistical tests for data in different levels of measurement considers tests for interval data.

5. PROGRAMMING TEST FOR INTERVAL DATA

Two tests for interval data will be covered in this chapter, one for two independent 2-sample data and one for 2 related samples. The arithmetic involved in the calculations involving all but small samples is particularly tedious when done by hand, as is well testified here and in Siegel, pp. 152-6 and pp. 88-92, where the arithmetic even for total data counts of 8 or 9 is heavy.

Randomization Test for 2 Independent Samples

This is the non-parametric equivalent of the parametric 't' test, without its assumptions that the data are drawn from populations with a normal distribution and that their variances are equal.

Under the null hypothesis of no difference in means, the association of any datum with one of the populations from which the samples were drawn is a matter of chance. An alternative hypothesis might be that the mean of a specified one of the populations is greater than that of the other. If there are N data altogether and r data in one group there are

$$^{N}C_{r} = \frac{N!}{(N-r)!\ r!}$$

possible arrangements ('combinations') of data in the two samples under the null hypothesis, Even with just 4 data in one group 5 in the other, this amounts to 126 possible arrangements. The test procedure is to count the number of arrangements which result in a lower mean data value in the sample hypothesized under H_1 having the lower mean. If a two-sided test is required, the number of arrangements which result also in a higher mean data value than that obtained must be included in the count. Then, the ratio of the count to the total number of possible arrangements gives the exact probability under the null hypothesis of the obtained arrangement of data.

For ease of hand calculation, suppose that the two small samples have the data values:

SAMPLE A   27 16 33 17

SAMPLE B   7   38 21

In this case there are nCr= 35 possible

arrangements, each of which has an equal probability of occurrence under the null hypothesis. The alternative hypothesis is that the mean of the population from which sample B was drawn has a lower mean. We count those arrangements of data which result in a lower mean than $(7+38+21)/3$ or equivalently those arrangements of data whose difference in sum $>= \Sigma A - \Sigma B = ((159-66)-66)=27$,

since $\Sigma A + \Sigma B = 159$.

The 35 possible arrangements and the differences in their sums are:

Sample B	Sample A	$\Sigma A - \Sigma B$
$7+16+17 = 40$	119	**79**
$7+16+21 = 44$	115	**71**
$7+16+27 = 50$	109	**59**
$7+16+33 = 56$	103	**47**
$7+16+38 = 61$	98	**37**
$7+17+21 = 45$	114	**69**
$7+17+27 = 51$	108	**57**
$7+17+33 = 57$	102	**45**
$7+17+38 = 62$	97	**35**

7+21+27 = 55	104	**49**
7+21+33 = 61	98	**37**
7+21+38 = 66	93	**27***
7+27+33 = 67	92	25
7+27+38 = 72	87	15
7+33+38 = 78	81	3
16+17+21 = 54	105	**51**
16+17+27 = 60	99	**39**
16+17+33 = 66	93	**27**
16+17+38 = 71	88	17
16+21+27 = 64	95	**31**
16+21+33 = 70	88	18
16+21+38 = 75	84	9
16+27+33 = 76	83	7
16+27+38 = 81	78	-3
16+33+38 = 87	72	-15
17+21+27 = 65	94	**29**
17+21+33 = 71	88	17
17+21+38 = 76	83	7
17+27+33 = 77	82	5

17+27+38 = 82	77	-15
17+33+38 = 88	71	-17
21+27+33 = 81	78	-3
21+27+38 = 86	73	-15
21+33+38 = 92	67	-25
27+33+38 = 98	61	*-37*

The starred entry is Sample A. The differences counted are emboldened.

Counting up,

p (H_0 : mean pop. A= mean pop. B; H_1 : mean pop. A>mean pop. B) =17/35.

Note that the entries counted are simply those which are >= ΣA =93, so this is all we need to consider in the program.

For a 2-sided test, we would have to count and include in the 2-sided probability of the data obtained in the samples all the arrangements in which $|\Sigma$A- ΣB$|$>27, which adds 1 more arrangement as can be seen from above (the entry is italicized).

The most straightforward approach, although cumbersome, is to re-calculate the sum for each arrangement, which, for the purposes of illustration and ease of programming, is done in the program shown on pp. 170-4, which calculates one-sided probabilities, with H_1 in the obtained direction. It does this by arranging the data in the largest (or equal largest) sample in a matrix which consists of one array per datum. For the above sample of 4 for example, the total of 7 data would be stored in a 4x4 matrix:

array				
d	38	33	27	21
c	33	27	21	17
b	27	21	17	16
a	21	17	16	7

(see lines 480-510 and 1260-1330 in the program print-out on pp. 170-4).

The data are in descending order in each array, and the data in each array is shifted one place to the right compared with the one below. The first two loops of a nested series of FOR-NEXT loops first generate all the possible data arrangements by varying the first two data in the lowest array. Then the process is repeated for the next array, then the next and so on, by incrementing and executing each higher loop. As a check that all possible combinations are considered, the program counts them in the variable NCK, an acronym for $^{n}C_{k}$.

As can be seen from the working above with just 4 data in one sample and 3 in the other, the amount of calculation involved is substantial and this rapidly increases for larger samples, the program taking longer and longer to come up with a result. So, it is only really useful for samples of data of manageable size.

However, the 't' test is a good approximation, given certain limiting conditions, where the total number of data >25. One of these conditions is that one sample should be no more than 5 times the size of the other. A second condition is that the kurtosis (peakiness) of the data set should not be too large. We will return to this topic in the next chapter which describes computer programs which estimate the values of some statistical properties of data distributions, including kurtosis. In fact, the 't' test approximation performed in the example below on a smaller set of 20 data gave a similar result to the exact figure of the randomization test.

Example

In the 1970's, a new design of oil-filled 275kV AC power cable was introduced. Previous testing had indicated superior ageing performance compared with conventional cables, and long-term data was collected to assess the performance of the new cable *in situ* against existing cables. For this purpose, 15 runs of the new cable were monitored against a control sample of 5 runs of conventional cable. The results (in years) are shown below:

CABLE LIFETIME (years)

New Cable	Conventional Cable
25.1	21.5
22.6	22.9
23.1	19.5
21.7	20.5
19.8	23.2
20.6	
24.8	
23.6	
22.6	
19.9	
26.4	
23.7	
24	
25.1	
20.8	

Table 15: Lifetime performance data of a 15 runs of a new design of 275kV cable compared with a control sample of 5 runs of conventional cable

Since lifetime data in this case were known from experience not to be normally distributed, a non-parametric test was decided upon to analyse the data. As the data were on an interval scale, the randomization test was chosen.

H_0 was that the populations from which the sample of lifetime data are drawn do not differ in mean.

H_1 was that the population from which the sample of lifetime data for the new cable was drawn has a higher mean.

The output of the program is shown below:

```
run_debug_basic_programs
Microsoft Windows [Version 6.0.6001]
Copyright (c) 2006 Microsoft Corporation.  All rights reserved.
c:\users\pejt4\basic_programs>RANDOMIZATION.BAS
ENTER THE NUMBERS OF DATA IN THE LARGEST SAMPLE (OR EQUAL LARGEST)? 15
ENTER THE NUMBER OF DATA IN THE SMALLEST (OR EQUAL SMALLEST) SAMPLE? 5
ENTER THE DATA IN THE LARGEST SAMPLE (OR EQUAL LARGEST)
? 25.1
? 22.6
? 23.1
? 21.7
? 19.8
? 20.6
? 24.8
? 23.6
? 22.6
? 19.9
? 26.4
? 23.7
? 24
? 25.1
? 20.8
ENTER THE DATA IN THE SMALLEST SAMPLE (OR EQUAL SMALLEST)
? 21.5
? 22.9
? 19.5
? 20.5
? 23.2

P (1 SIDED) .0873323
```

The exact probability of the sample data under H_0 is 0.087, and so under H_0 $0.05 < p < 0.1$. By comparison, a 't' test gave an associated one-sided probability of 0.072. It was decided that the results were inconclusive and that further performance monitoring of the new cable was required.

Randomization Test for Two Related Samples

This test is useful for matched samples and 'before and after' measures in matched pair designs, where the data are on an interval scale, but do not necessarily conform to a normal distribution. The data for this test consist of *differences*, with sign. The null hypothesis is that, given the differences in size in the 'before and after' data, the direction of the differences (+ or -) obtained are chance variations. Under the null hypothesis, the sign of any one difference is just as likely as the other sign, and if there are N pairs of data, the possible 2^N arrangements of signs are all equally likely. H_0 is tested by counting the number of arrangements whose sum is as great or greater than that obtained, and comparing this with the total number of possible arrangements.

In the program whose print-out is shown on pp. 175-6, the rationale for providing this count is very similar to that used for the randomization test for independent samples, namely, to generate each possible arrangement in turn and test its sum against the sum of the obtained data. The one-sided probability given should be doubled for a 2-sided test. Since only one set of data is involved in testing, each arrangement simply involves reversing the sign of one datum and no ranking is required, the related samples randomization test program is much shorter and simpler than the independent samples version. However, the same remarks addressed to limitations due to the amount of calculation required for larger samples apply to both tests. But again, where N>25, a good approximation is available, given certain limiting conditions. This a normal approximation with a mean of zero and standard deviation equal to the standard deviation of the data from zero.

Example

The wear-reducing properties of a new synthetic polymer- based lubricating oil in industrial scale wind turbine gearboxes was to be compared with conventional lubricating oil. The wind turbines to be used in the test were all in the same wind farm, were the same age, of the same manufacture and the same rated output, and so a related 2-sample design was appropriate. The gearboxes of 2 samples of 13 wind turbines were drained and flushed. One sample's gearboxes were filled with synthetic oil, the other's with conventional oil. After a suitable period of operation, the mass of metal particulate matter (from the gears, bearings and shafts produced by abrasion, impact, etc. during running) in the residues of the drained and filtered oil from each turbine was measured. Differences in these measures, with signs, for pairs of wind turbines, one from each sample selected at random, constitute the data of the test. The results obtained (in grams) are shown below:

MASS OF METAL PARTICULATE (g)		Difference
synthetic polymer-based oil	conventional oil	
1706	1131	-575
1755	1148	607
1579	1797	-218
1923	1584	339
1650	1633	17
1295	1361	-66
1707	1522	-185
1311	2073	-762
1888	1874	14
1264	1932	-668
1995	1538	457
1570	1548	22
1829	1840	-11

Table 16: Mass of metal particulate matter in synthetic polymer based and conventional wind turbine gearbox oils

No convincing data was yet available about the wear-reducing properties of the synthetic polymer oil, and so a 2-sided hypothesis was tested; and as no distributional assumptions about the data were made, the related samples randomization test was chosen for the analysis.

The output of the program after entering the difference data in the above table was as follows:

```
run_debug_basic_programs
c:\users\pejt4\Basic_programs>RANDOMIZATION_RM.BAS
HOW MANY PAIRS OF DATA?
? 13
ENTER THE *difference* DATA FOR EACH MATCHED PAIR, WITH sign IF NEGATIVE
? -575
? 607
? -218
? 339
? 17
? -66
? 185
? -762
? 14
? -668
? 457
? 22
? -11
P (1-SIDED)= .6672363

c:\users\pejt4\Basic_programs>_
```

The high probability returned indicates that the differences in wear properties of the synthetic polymer-based and conventional oils in terms of metal particulate matter produced in wind turbine gearboxes running in oil are no are no less (and no more) than would be expected by chance.

It is interesting to note that in fact these particular data are quite likely to have been drawn from a normally distributed population: a two- sided 't' test of the null hypothesis that the mean difference is zero returns an associated probability of 0.670- very close to the figure obtained from the randomization test. Consequently, the normal approximation also gave a two-sided probability close to that obtained in the randomization test:

The standard deviation of differences from a zero mean is 1461.8, and the sum of differences is -659. Now

$$z = \frac{\Sigma \text{ differences} - \text{mean}}{\text{standard deviation}}$$

and so z = -659/1461.8 = -.45 with an associated 2-sided probability of 0.653.

6. PROGRAMMING STATISTICAL MEASURES OF SOME PROPERTIES OF DATA DISTRIBUTIONS

In the last chapter we saw that normality of the distribution of the population from which the sample of data to be tested is drawn is an important consideration in the decision as to whether non-parametric tests should be used instead of, normally first-choice, parametric tests. In was noted that non-parametric tests such as the chi-square test, the sign test and the median test tend to be less powerful than the corresponding parametric tests, though the Mann-Whitney 'U' test, Wilcoxon matched pairs signed ranks test and Kruskal-Wallis one way ANOVAR are nearly as powerful and the two randomization tests and the Friedman 2 way ANOVA can be virtually equal in power to the most powerful of the equivalent parametric tests (the 't' and F tests). In this chapter, we will look at some measures of the properties of data distributions and their computerisation in *BASIC*.

The Mode and Modal Class

<u>Mode</u>

The mode is strictly speaking defined as *the* most frequently occurring datum value in a data set. So that if a set of data contains more than one datum with the highest frequency then it has no mode.

For example, consider the data set below:

14 22 19 16 25 33 12 17 22 19 33 17 20 22 27

33

Two data values- 22 and 33- occur most frequently (with a frequency of 3).

However, whereas as a normal distribution of data has a single mode, other data distributions, like one above, may be referred to as bi-modal (having two modes).

If all the data values are different, then there is no mode.

These features are incorporated in the *BASIC* program whose print-out is shown on pp. 177-8. The first part of the program ranks the data and prints out an ordered list. Since equal data values in the set are grouped together in the list, it is easy to see how many data are of a given value and which, if any is the most frequent. Line 390 counts the frequency of each datum which occurs more than once. The most frequent count is in b(1) and after all the data are processed b(1)=0 there is 'no mode' (line 510). Otherwise, the most frequent datum or data are printed out. Note in line 555 that if there is a single most frequently occurring datum C=1, which, if passed onto the FOR-NEXT loop beginning line 560 would, in V*intbas BASIC,* cause an error in the calculated mode, because the loop would count down instead of up (since C-1 would be zero).

For completeness, the other two averages, the mean and the median of the data set are also displayed.

Example

A print-out of the output of the program using the above data set is shown below:

```
run_debug_basic_programs
Microsoft Windows [Version 6.0.6001]
Copyright (c) 2006 Microsoft Corporation.  All rights reserved.


RANKED DATA:

  12            14            16            17            17            19
  33            33            19            20            22            22
  22            25            27            33

MODE:
  22    33

MEDIAN 19.5
MEAN 21.9375

c:\users\pejt4\Basic_programs>_
```

Modal Class

If the data is in the form of a histogram it will be necessary to estimate the mode. One method (see Graham and Graham (1988), pp. 46-7) is based on the *modal class* of the histogram, i.e., the class with the highest frequency and the frequencies of adjacent classes. An example is shown below.

The modal class is 50-59, with the highest frequency of 9 marks. The class adjacent to the modal class to the left is 40-49 with a frequency of 6 marks, and the class adjacent to the modal class to the right is 60-69 with a frequency of 5 marks.

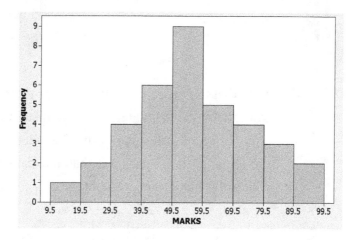

Fig. 1: Histogram showing the frequency of marks gained by 36 individuals in a test (*Data Source: Graham and Graham (1988))*

We now need to estimate how far into the modal class the mode lies. This is given by:

Modal class lower boundary +

$$\frac{\text{(modal class frequency-frequency of adjacent class to the left)}}{\text{(modal class frequency-frequency of adjacent class to the left)} + \text{(modal class frequency-frequency of adjacent class to the right)}} \times \text{class interval}$$

which in this case is

$$49.5 + \frac{3}{3+4} \times 10$$

$= 54.$

The data set from which the histogram was produced, after processing by the previous program, is a follows:

```
RANKED DATA:
12  22  25  31  34  34  39  41  44  45  45  48  49  50  51  51  52  55  56  56  56
58  66  67  68  68  69  70  73  74  76  81  84  85  92  98
```

Note that the mode is 56, which is slightly different from the mode estimated from the histogram of the data, because information in the data is lost in grouping it (it is assumed that the data set from which the histogram was obtained is not available for analysis).

To extend the mode program to cater for finding an estimated mode from a histogram, lines were added to the program to give the user an option to enter histogram information. Further lines were added to perform the arithmetic in the above expression to find the mode from the modal class. The extension to the program is shown on p. 178.

To make the operation of the extension to the program clear, the input and output using information from the histogram on p. 111 is shown below:

```
run_debug_basic_programs
Microsoft Windows [Version 6.0.6001]
Copyright (c) 2006 Microsoft Corporation.  All rights reserved.

c:\users\pejt4\Basic_programs>MODE1.BAS
PRESS [1] TO CALCULATE MODE FROM A HISTOGRAM; [2] FROM A DATA SET? 1
OF THE HISTOGRAM:

ENTER THE CLASS INTERVAL? 10
ENTER THE LOWER BOUNDARY OF MODAL CLASS? 49.5
ENTER THE FREQUENCY OF THE MODAL CLASS? 9
ENTER THE FREQUENCY OF THE CLASS TO THE left OF THE MODAL CLASS? 6
ENTER THE FREQUENCY OF THE CLASS TO THE right OF THE MODAL CLASS? 5
MODE (estimated):
 54

c:\users\pejt4\Basic_programs>
```

Skewness and Kurtosis

Skewness

The normal distribution is symmetrical about the mean- the portion of the distribution to the left of the data axis is a reflection in the frequency axis of the portion of the distribution to the right of the data axis:

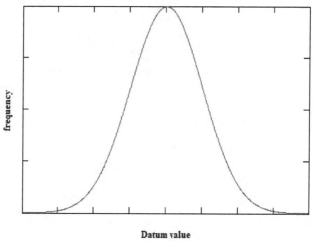

Datum value

Fig. 2: A Normal distribution

The following distribution is asymmetrical with a long 'tail' in the direction of the positive data axis

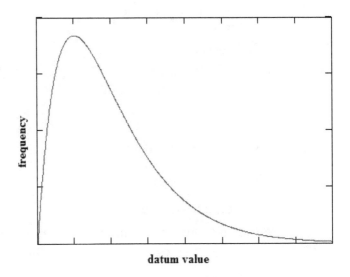

Fig. 3: A Positively skewed distribution

Distributions may also be skewed in the direction of the negative data axis (negatively skewed).

Prior to deciding to use a non-parametric ANOVAR test in preference to a (parametric) F-test in the analysis of the 30 test scores on pp. 57-8, the following histogram of the data was produced:

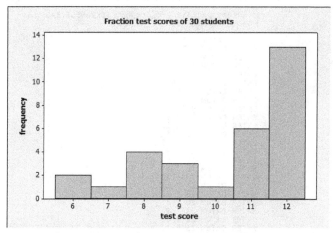

Fig. 4: Histogram of 30 test scores in Trigger (1985)

The deviation in the shape of this histogram from what might be expected of a sample from a normal distribution warranted further investigation in the form of an estimate of the skewness of the distribution from which the obtained sample was drawn.

The program whose print-out is shown on p. 179 calculates a measure of the skewness of a data distribution from a formula in *Genstat*, together with its standard error (S.E.). The input and output of the program using the data in Table7, is shown below:

116

```
run_debug_basic_programs
Microsoft Windows [Version 6.0.6001]
Copyright (c) 2006 Microsoft Corporation.  All rights reserved.

c:\users\pejt4\Basic_programs>SKEWNESS.BAS
HOW MANY DATA? 30

ENTER DATUM 1 ? 8
ENTER DATUM 2 ? 11
ENTER DATUM 3 ? 6
ENTER DATUM 4 ? 12
ENTER DATUM 5 ? 12
ENTER DATUM 6 ? 8
ENTER DATUM 7 ? 11
ENTER DATUM 8 ? 7
ENTER DATUM 9 ? 9
ENTER DATUM 10 ? 12
ENTER DATUM 11 ? 11
ENTER DATUM 12 ? 11
ENTER DATUM 13 ? 11
ENTER DATUM 14 ? 6
ENTER DATUM 15 ? 9
ENTER DATUM 16 ? 8
ENTER DATUM 17 ? 12
ENTER DATUM 18 ? 12
ENTER DATUM 19 ? 12
ENTER DATUM 20 ? 8
ENTER DATUM 21 ? 9
ENTER DATUM 22 ? 12
ENTER DATUM 23 ? 12
ENTER DATUM 24 ? 12
ENTER DATUM 25 ? 12
ENTER DATUM 26 ? 10
ENTER DATUM 27 ? 11
ENTER DATUM 28 ? 12
ENTER DATUM 29 ? 12
ENTER DATUM 30 ? 12
SKEWNESS:-.8733089 S.E. : .44136742
```

Notice that the skewness is negative and almost 2 standard errors from zero, indicating a probable lack of normality in the distribution from which the sample of data was drawn.

Kurtosis

Kurtosis refers to the extent of 'peakiness' (or flatness) in the data distribution. A leptokurtic (peaky) distribution is shown below:

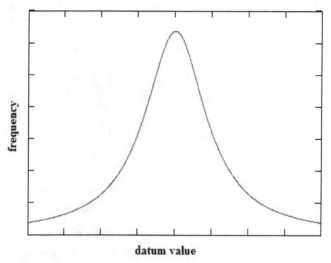

Fig. 5: A (lepto-) Kurtic Distribution

In discussing the Randomization test for two independent samples, the possible use of a 't' test for data sets larger than 25 was considered, and the condition was mentioned that the kurtosis of the sample 'should be not be too large'. An extension to the skewness program which adds lines to calculate a measure of kurtosis and its standard error is shown on p. 179.

Table 15 contains the data used in the example illustrating the test, and a histogram of the data follows:

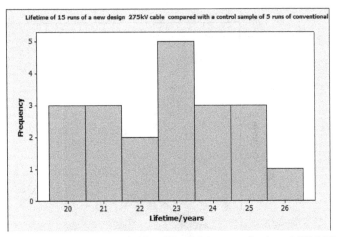

Fig. 6: Lifetime of 15 runs of a new design 275 kV cable compared with control sample of 5 runs of conventional cable

The histogram indicates a possible platykurtosis in the data distribution, and so the data sample was entered into the extended skewness program to obtain measures of kurtosis and skewness. The input and output is shown below:

```
run_debug_basic_programs
Microsoft Windows [Version 6.0.6001]
Copyright (c) 2006 Microsoft Corporation.

c:\users\pejt4\Basic_programs>SKEWNESS.BAS
HOW MANY DATA? 20

ENTER DATUM 1 ? 25.1
ENTER DATUM 2 ? 22.6
ENTER DATUM 3 ? 23.1
ENTER DATUM 4 ? 21.7
ENTER DATUM 5 ? 19.8
ENTER DATUM 6 ? 20.6
ENTER DATUM 7 ? 24.8
ENTER DATUM 8 ? 23.6
ENTER DATUM 9 ? 22.6
ENTER DATUM 10 ? 19.9
ENTER DATUM 11 ? 26.4
ENTER DATUM 12 ? 23.7
ENTER DATUM 13 ? 24
ENTER DATUM 14 ? 25.1
ENTER DATUM 15 ? 20.8
ENTER DATUM 16 ? 21.5
ENTER DATUM 17 ? 22.9
ENTER DATUM 18 ? 19.5
ENTER DATUM 19 ? 20.5
ENTER DATUM 20 ? 23.2
SKEWNESS: .08522305 S.E. : .5383819
KURTOSIS:-.9660864 S.E.: .9923836
```

The output evidences little skewness but some degree of platykurtosis (flattening of the distribution) as expected from the histogram. Nevertheless, this is not serious enough to affect the result of the 't' test which, as previously noted, is in close agreement with that of the randomization test, in spite of a sample size smaller than 25.

7. SUMMARY AND CONCLUSION

Summary

This book has shown how non-parametric tests can be computerised in the *BASIC* programming language of the late 1970's and 1980's.

In Chapter 1, after a brief discussion of the use of non-parametric tests as alternatives to parametric tests, hypothesis testing, and the concepts of power and degrees of freedom were outlined.

Chapter 2 considered the various levels of data measurement in terms of the amount of information carried, from categorical or nominal data through ranked data to interval and ratio data, with examples, and the permissible arithmetical operations on each which might be performed in calculating the test statistic in an appropriate test.

The number of samples analysed- 1, 2, or more and the relatedness of the samples-whether each sample of data is independently chosen or is matched in some way were discussed prior to describing how these features could be used to classify non-parametric tests. From this emerged a table showing the hierachical order of tests to be covered in chapters 3-5, starting with tests designed for nominal data in Chapter 3, and moving on to tests designed for ordinal data in Chapter 4 and finally to tests designed for interval data in chapter 5. In each chapter, one or more tests for each of the one, two and k-sample cases, for each of independent samples (including appropriate correlation tests) and related sample designs were featured, and their programming in *BASIC* outlined. Examples of their use to test hypotheses and the output of the resulting computer program on example data sets, were described. The example data sets were mostly drawn from the author's Ph.D research or her work on electricity generation for recent books on the subject.

Where appropriate, normal approximations for sufficiently large samples were incorporated in the computer programs or a parametric alternative was described.

Chapter 3 described the rationale of the Binomial test and one sample Chi-square test, and how the calculation of the associated test statistic was programmed in *BASIC*. For the two-sample case, the Contingency correlation test of association was described. Chapter 3 then showed how the one sample chi-square test program was modified for 2 independent samples of data, and then covered the programming of the Fisher Exact test, particularly useful where the frequency of data in one or more categories is too low for chi-square testing. The McNemar test was the featured test for the 2 related sample case. The last section of Chapter 3 considered tests for k-sample nominal data, beginning with the k-sample chi-square test. Finally the CochranQ extension of the McNemar test forming the basis of the program for k related samples was outlined.

It was noted that the power of tests designed for nominal data to reject the null hypothesis when it is false can be considerably less than for the corresponding parametric tests where they exist (meaning that considerably larger samples are required for a given significance level). The tests covered in the following chapter offer a power advantage over tests designed for nominal data, given the higher information content of suitable ordinal data.

Chapter 4 began with a description of the rationale of the test and discussed the *BASIC* program for the Kolomogorov-Smirnov one sample goodness of fit test. Suitable if the data can be ranked, it was noted that this test is a more powerful alternative to the one sample chi-squared test and can be used for small samples not suitable for the chi-square test. If the data are not ranked, the second test described for the one sample case for ordinal data, the runs test, may be used where each datum can be rated as 'above' 'below' or equal according on some criterion, which might be the median of the data set, for example.

Chapter 4 went on to discuss the 2-sample case for ordinal data beginning with the Spearman correlation test for ranked data. The discussion described how the associated computer program makes a correction for ties and determines the statistical significance of the Spearman correlation coefficient under the null hypothesis of no association. The power of the test was noted to be 91% when compared with the equivalent parametric (Pearson correlation) test.

In the two independent samples category, the median test program enables data sets to be compared to test the likelihood that the samples come from populations with the same median: Chapter 4 described the ranking of the data in the two samples and their assignment to one of the two groups above or below the grand median, the production of the corresponding contingency table and the application of the 2 sample chi-square test to it.

However, the median test wastes information compared with the Mann-Whitney 'U' test, a computerised version of which was described, which compared with a 't' test has a power approaching 95%, compared with 63% for the median test. Furthermore, it was noted that a good normal approximation is available as an alternative for sample sizes as small as 8.

In the related 2-samples category, the use of the Binomial test program was to determine the probability associated with the obtained number of matched data pairs in which the datum of sample A>sample B, was described. Again, like the Median test, the sign test wastes power, but the Wilcoxon matched pairs signed ranks test and the computerised version described in the text achieves a power of 95% compared with the 't' test, whereas the sign test only manages 63%. And also, again, a normal approximation may be used with larger data sets.

For the k-sample case, the computerisation of the Concordance test of association between several characteristics of more than two samples was described for data which are ranked. It was noted that the Concordance test statistic W is a good approximation to chi-square for sample sizes of 8 and more, from which the Spearman correlation coefficient for each pair of samples can be obtained.

For k independent samples, a *BASIC* program for the Kruskal-Wallis one way Analysis of Variance was described, as an alternative to the F test parametric ANOVAR, compared with which it has a power of over 95%.

Lastly in Chapter 4, in the k-related samples category, the computerisation in *BASIC* of the Friedman 2 way analysis of variance was discussed. Like the Kruskal-Wallis Analysis of Variance test, this produces a test statistic which, for sample sizes which are not too small, is a good approximation to chi-square, and so the program instructions used for the chi-square test could be used in the program for the Friedman 2-way ANOVAR test once the ranks for each sample on each characteristic were assigned. It was noted that the latter is another powerful test, rivalling that of the corresponding parametric ANOVAR.

The final chapter concerned with computerized statistical tesing, Chapter 5, covers two tests for 2-sample interval data. The power of these tests are 100% given that they provide exact probabilities and all of the information in the data is used. Based on their rationales, the *BASIC* programs for these randomization tests were described as working by generating and counting all possible arrangements or *combinations* of the sample data values considered as equally likely under the null hypothesis, and then determining what fraction of these are as extreme or more extreme than the samples obtained. However, it was concluded that the *BASIC* programming environment in these cases was best suited to moderately small samples, since the number of arrangements involved for bigger samples could be very large (for example two independent samples with 12 data in one and 13 in other gives rise to NCR = 25C12= 5 200 300 combinations).

However, provided that the data in larger samples satisfied certain data distribution or relative sample size properties, it was shown how a normal approximation or a 't' test might be used as an alternative.

Finally Chapter 6 looked at some measures of the properties of data distributions- notably the mode, skewness and kurtosis, and their computerisation in *BASIC*.

Conclusion

In computerising the statistical tests and measures described in this book, the author found the simple to understand   instructions of *BASIC* and their organisation in lines of statements executed in numbered order eased the task of casting the rationale of the test into the logic of a computer program and couching the calculations involved in terms of the expressions allowed by the language. The *BASIC* language facilitated the author's quest to write her own programs to make the non-parametric tests described in Siegel available in a form which not only take the tedium out of the hand calculations involved in paper and pencil methods, but enable more realistic data sets to analysed.

At first, this was achieved on a microcomputer word processor running a 1980's version of *BASIC*. But the program-editing environment and improvement in program execution speed when the author worked on transferring these programs to a modern *Windows* computer with a GHz processor running the 'old fashioned' *BASIC*, was a revelation. The graphics user interface of *Windows* compared with the microcomputer's restriction to command line, with the highlighting, cutting and pasting facilities available in Notepad, made the 'mechanical' aspects of writing, re-ordering and correcting the lines of the program much easier and almost a joy by comparison.

The speed advantage was to become crucial with the last two (randomization test) programs, the *Windows* versions of the programs returning a result for moderately sized data sets in matter of seconds, which would take hours on the microcomputer version with its slow kHz processor speed.

In comparing the two *BASIC* programming environments, the only drawback felt of the *Windows Vintbas BASIC* environment was the lack of an *immediate execution* mode, which during the original programming had enabled the author to check on the values of important variables used in the program after the program has been executed, and as mentioned earlier, enabled sections of the program to be tested independently, 'live'. This would work even if there were bugs elsewhere in the program, which could therefore be temporarily ignored. In the *Windows Vintbas BASIC* environment, resort had to be had to inserting PRINT statements at strategic places in the program to print out the value(s) of the variable(s) concerned, and re-executing the program each time any alteration to the program had been made in order to see the result. And of course, if there were fatal bugs anywhere in the program, these would have to be sorted out first before the program would run at all. Even if the program did run, execution of the whole program could introduce more sources of obfuscating error.

The limitations of *BASIC* only became apparent when very large amounts of calculation were involved in the program. Returning to the two randomization test programs, the author found that *BASIC* interpreter was overwhelmed by data sets of more than 20 in one program and 13 in the other.

But when the randomization test for independent samples program was re-written in *Borland TurboC* compiler, data sets up 25 (beyond which a normal approximation is appropriate) were manageable. The use of *BASIC* programs as a 'stepping stone' onto computerisation in *Borland TurboC* of complex tasks such as higher order complex matrix inversion, higher order simultaneous equation and polynomial equation solving is the subject the next volume of this series.

8. APPENDICES

Print-out of the Binomial test program

```
bintest - Notepad

File   Edit   Format   View   Help

10 REM***BINOMIAL STATISTICAL TEST FOR ONE SAMPLE OF NOMINAL DATA
20 ?"ENTER THE OBSERVED FREQUENCY IN CATEGORY 1";
30 INPUT O(1)
40 ?"ENTER THE EXPECTED FREQUENCY IN CATEGORY 1";
50 INPUT E(1)
60 ?"ENTER THE OBSERVED FREQUENCY IN CATEGORY 2";
70 INPUT O(2)
80 ?"ENTER THE EXPECTED FREQUENCY IN CATEGORY 2";
90 INPUT E(2)
91 N=O(1)+O(2)
92 P=E(1)/N:X=O(1)
95 ?"FIND PROBABILITY THAT >=";O(1);"EXPECTED PRESS [1]"
98?"FIND PROBABILITY THAT <=";O(1);"EXPECTED PRESS [2]";
99 INPUT S:IF S<>1 THEN S=-1:A=X:B=0
100REM
110 ?:?:?:?:?:?:?:?:?:?:?:?:?:?
120 ?"THE CONTINGENCY TABLE OF FREQUENCIES IS:":?:?
130 ?,"OBSERVED","EXPECTED"
140 ?:?"CATEGORY 1",O(1),E(1)
150 ?"CATEGORY 2",O(2),E(2):?
160 ? "TOTAL",O(1)+O(2),E(1)+E(2)
170 ?:?
180REM
190 REM
200 REM
210 IF N>33 THEN ? "Z=";(X-N*P)/(SQR(N*P*(1-P)))
215 REM NORMAL APPROXIMATION
220 K=N:GOSUB 300:NFACT=Y
225 GOSUB 230
227 GOTO 280
230 FOR I=A TO X STEP S
240 k=I:GOSUB 300:XFACT=Y
250 K=N-I:GOSUB 300:NXFACT=Y
260 SUM=SUM+(NFACT/(XFACT*NXFACT))*P^I*(1-P)^(N-I)
270 NEXT I
275 RETURN
280 ? "P=";SUM
290 STOP
300 Y=1
310 IF K=0 THEN 350
320 FOR J=1 TO K
330 Y=Y*J
340 NEXT J
350 RETURN
```

Print-out of the Chi-square One sample test program

```
CHISQONE - Notepad
File  Edit  Format  View  Help
2.706,3.841,6.635,4.605,5.991,9.210,6.251,7.815,11.341,7.779,9.488,13.277,9.236,11.070,15.086
130 DATA
10.645,12.592,16.812,12.017,14.067,18.475,13.362,15.507,20.090,14.684,16.919,21.666,15.987,1
8.307,23.209
140 DATA
17.275,19.675,24.725,18.549,21.026,26.217,19.812,22.362,27.688,21.064,23.685,29.141,22.307,2
4.996,30.578
150 DATA
23.542,26.296,32.000,24.769,27.587,33.409,25.989,28.869,34.805,27.204,30.144,36.191,28.412,
31.410,37.566
160 DATA
29.615,32.671,38.932,30.813,33.924,40.289,32.007,35.172,41.638,33.196,36.415,42.980,34.382,3
7.652,44.314
170 DATA
35.563,38.885,45.642,36.741,40.113,46.963,37.916,41.337,48.278,39.087,42.557,49.588,40.256,
43.773,50.892
180 FOR I=1 TO 30
190 READ A(I),B(I),C(I)
200 NEXT I
210 ?"ENTER THE NUMBER OF SAMPLES";
220 INPUT M
230 IF M=1 THEN 860
860 ?"ENTER THE NUMBER OF CATEGORIES (MAX=30)";
870 INPUT N:IF N>30 THEN ?"MUST BE <= 30":STOP
880 M=3
890 DIM O(N):DIM E(N)
900 FOR I=1 TO N
910 ?"ENTER THE OBSERVED FREQUENCY IN CATEGORY";I
920 INPUT O(I)
930 ?"ENTER THE EXPECTED FREQUENCY IN CATEGORY";I
940 INPUT E(I)
950 IF E(I)<5 THEN ?:?:?:?"OBSERVED FREQUENCY MUST BE 5 OR MORE":STOP
960 NEXT I
970 ?:?:?:?:?:?:?:?:?
980 ?"THE CONTINGENCY TABLE OF FREQUENCIES IS;"
990 ?
1000 ?"CATEGORY","OBSERVED","EXPECTED"
1010 ?
1020 FOR I=1 TO N
1030 ?I,O(I),E(I)
1040 NEXT I
1050 ?"--------------------------------------------------------------------"
1060 FOR I=1 TO N
1070 X=X+O(I)
1080 Y=Y+E(I)
1090 NEXT I
1100 ?"   TOTAL",X,Y
1110 FOR I=1 TO N
1120 Z=Z+(O(I)-E(I))^2/E(I)
1130 NEXT I
1140 ?:?:Y=INT(Z)
1150 Z=Z-INT(Z)
```

```
1160 Z=Z*10^M
1170 Z=INT(Z+.5)
1180 Z=Z/10^M
1190 Z=Z+Y
1200 ?"CHI-SQUARE=";Z
1210 ? N-1;"DEGREE(S) OF FREEDOM"
1220 ?:?"H(0):";
1230 IF Z=C(N-1) THEN ?"P=0.01":STOP
1240 IF Z>C(N-1) THEN ?"P<0.01":STOP
1250 IF Z=B(N-1) THEN ?"P=0.05":STOP
1260 IF Z>B(N-1) THEN ?"0.05>P>0.01":STOP
1270 IF Z=A(N-1) THEN ?"P=0.1":STOP
1280 IF Z<B(N-1) THEN ?"P>0.1":STOP
1290 IF Z>A(N-1) THEN ?"0.1>P>0.05":STOP
```

Print-out of the Chi-square Two sample test program

```
CHISQTWO - Notepad
File  Edit  Format  View  Help
100 REM***CALCULATES CHI-SQUARE STATISTIC FOR TWO SAMPLE NOMINAL DATA
110 DIM A(30):DIM B(30):DIM C(30)
120 DATA
2.706,3.841,6.635,4.605,5.991,9.210,6.251,7.815,11.341,7.779,9.488,13.277,9.236,11.070,15.086
130 DATA
10.645,12.592,16.812,12.017,14.067,18.475,13.362,15.507,20.090,14.684,16.919,21.666,15.987,1
8.307,23.209
140 DATA
17.275,19.675,24.725,18.549,21.026,26.217,19.812,22.362,27.688,21.064,23.685,29.141,22.307,2
4.996,30.578
150 DATA
23.542,26.296,32.000,24.769,27.587,33.409,25.989,28.869,34.805,27.204,30.144,36.191,28.412,
31.410,37.566
160 DATA
29.615,32.671,38.932,30.813,33.924,40.289,32.007,35.172,41.638,33.196,36.415,42.980,34.382,3
7.652,44.314
170 DATA
35.563,38.885,45.642,36.741,40.113,46.963,37.916,41.337,48.278,39.087,42.557,49.588,40.256,
43.773,50.892
180 FOR I=1 TO 30
190 READ A(I),B(I),C(I)
200 NEXT I
210 ?"ENTER THE NUMBER OF SAMPLES";
220 INPUT M
230 REM
240 IF M<>2 THEN ?"MUST BE TWO SAMPLES":STOP
245 ?"ENTER THE NUMBER OF CATEGORIES";
250 INPUT N
260 DIM O1(N+1,3):DIM E1(N+1,3)
270 FOR I=1 TO N
280 FOR J=1 TO 2
290 ?"ENTER THE FREQUENCY IN CATEGORY";I;"SAMPLE";J
300 INPUT O1(I,J)
310 NEXT J
320 NEXT I
330 FOR J=1 TO 2:REM CALCULATE COLUMN TOTALS
340 FOR I=1 TO N
350 O1(N+1,J)=O1(N+1,J)+O1(I,J)
360 E1(N+1,J)=O1(N+1,J)
370 NEXT I
380 NEXT J
390 FOR I=1 TO N:REM CALCULATE ROW TOTALS
400 FOR J=1 TO 2
410 O1(I,3)=O1(I,3)+O1(I,J)
420 E1(I,3)=O1(I,3)
430 NEXT J
440 NEXT I
450 FOR I=1 TO N
460 X=X+O1(I,3)
470 O1(N+1,3)=X:REM GRAND TOTAL
480 NEXT I
490 FOR I=1 TO N
```

```
500 FOR J=1 TO 2
510 E1(I,J)=O1(N+1,J)*O1(i,3)/X:REM CALCULATE EXPECTED FREQUENCIES
520 NEXT J
530 NEXT I
540 ?:?:?:?:?:?:?:?:?
550 ? TAB(16) "SAMPLE":REM PRINT OUT CONTINGENCY TABLE
560 FOR I=1 TO 2
570 ? TAB (10*I);I;
580 NEXT I
590 ? TAB(10*I+9) "TOTAL (O/E)";
600 ?
610 ? "CATEGORY"
620 FOR I=1 TO N+1
630 FOR J=1 TO 3
640 IF J=1 AND I<>N+1 THEN ?"   ";I;"O";:REM OMIT "O" FROM "TOTAL" LINE
650 IF J=1 AND I=N+1 THEN ?TAB(7);"TOTAL (O/E)";
660 ? TAB(10+10*J);O1(I,J);
670 NEXT J
680 ?
690 FOR J=1 TO 3
700 IF J=1 AND I<>N+1 THEN ?"   ";I;"E";
710 IF I<>N+1 THEN ?TAB(10+10*J);E1(I,J);
720 NEXT J
730 ?:?
740 NEXT I
750 ? TAB(30) "O: OBSERVED FREQUENCY"
760 ? TAB(30) "E:  EXPECTED FREQUENCY"
770 IF N=2 THEN Z=O1(3,3)*(ABS(O1(1,1)*O1(2,2)-O1(1,2)*O1(2,1))-O1(3,3)/2)^2/(O1(3,1)
*O1(3,2)*O1(2,3)*O1(1,3)):GOTO 830
780 FOR I=1 TO N
780 FOR I=1 TO N
790 FOR J=1 TO 2
800 Z=Z+(O1(I,J)-E1(I,J))^2/E1(I,J)
810 NEXT j
820 NEXT I
830 ?:?"CHI-SQUARE=";Z
840 N=(N-1)*(M-1):GOTO 1220:REM CALCULATE DEGREES OF FREEDOM
860 ?"ENTER THE NUMBER OF CATEGORIES (MAX=30)";
870 INPUT N:IF N>30 THEN ?"MUST BE <= 30":STOP
880 M=3
890 DIM O(N):DIM E(N)
900 FOR I=1 TO N
910 ?"ENTER THE OBSERVED FREQUENCY IN CATEGORY";I
920 INPUT O(I)
930 ?"ENTER THE EXPECTED FREQUENCY IN CATEGORY";I
940 INPUT E(I)
950 IF E(I)<5 THEN ?:?:?:?:?"OBSERVED FREQUENCY MUST BE 5 OR MORE":STOP
960 NEXT I
970 ?:?:?:?:?:?:?:?:?:?
980 ?"THE CONTINGENCY TABLE OF FREQUENCIES IS;"
990 ?
1000 ?"CATEGORY","OBSERVED","EXPECTED"
1010 ?
1020 FOR I=1 TO N
1030 ?I,O(I),E(I)
1040 NEXT I
1050 ?"----------------------------------------------------------------------------"
1060 FOR I=1 TO N
1070 X=X+O(I)
1080 Y=Y+E(I)
```

```
1090 NEXT I
1100 ?"  TOTAL",X,Y
1110 FOR I=1 TO N
1120 Z=Z+(O(I)-E(I))^2/E(I)
1130 NEXT I
1140 ?:?:Y=INT(Z)
1150 Z=Z-INT(Z)
1160 Z=Z*10^M
1170 Z=INT(Z+.5)
1180 Z=Z/10^M
1190 Z=Z+Y
1200 ?"CHI-SQUARE=";Z
1210 ? N-1;"DEGREE(S) OF FREEDOM"
1220 ?:?"H(0):";
1230 IF Z=C(N-1) THEN ?"P=0.01":STOP
1240 IF Z>C(N-1) THEN ?"P<0.01":STOP
1250 IF Z=B(N-1) THEN ?"P=0.05":STOP
1260 IF Z>B(N-1) THEN ?"0.05>P>0.01":STOP
1270 IF Z=A(N-1) THEN ?"P=0.1":STOP
1280 IF Z<B(N-1) THEN ?"P>0.1":STOP
1290 IF Z>A(N-1) THEN ?"0.1>P>0.05":STOP
```

Print-out of the Contingency test program

```
100 REM***CONTINGENCY  TEST  OF THE SIGNIFANCE OF THE COORELATION BETWEEN
2 SETS OF CATEGORICAL (NOMINAL) DATA
110 DIM A(30):DIM B(30):DIM C(30)
120 DATA
2.706,3.841,6.635,4.605,5.991,9.210,6.251,7.815,11.341,7.779,9.488,13.277,9.236,11.070,15.086
130 DATA
10.645,12.592,16.812,12.017,14.067,18.475,13.362,15.507,20.090,14.684,16.919,21.666,15.987,1
8.307,23.209
140 DATA
17.275,19.675,24.725,18.549,21.026,26.217,19.812,22.362,27.688,21.064,23.685,29.141,22.307,2
4.996,30.578
150 DATA
23.542,26.296,32.000,24.769,27.587,33.409,25.989,28.869,34.805,27.204,30.144,36.191,28.412,
31.410,37.566
160 DATA
29.615,32.671,38.932,30.813,33.924,40.289,32.007,35.172,41.638,33.196,36.415,42.980,34.382,3
7.652,44.314
170 DATA
35.563,38.885,45.642,36.741,40.113,46.963,37.916,41.337,48.278,39.087,42.557,49.588,40.256,
43.773,50.892
180 FOR I=1 TO 30
190 READ A(I),B(I),C(I)
200 NEXT I
210 ?"ENTER THE NUMBER OF CATEGORIES IN SET 1";
220 INPUT M
230 REM
240 IF M=1 THEN ?"MUST AT LEAST  TWO CATEGORIES":STOP
245 ?"ENTER THE NUMBER OF CATEGORIES IN SET 2";
250 INPUT N
260 DIM O1(N+1,M+1):DIM E1(N+1,M+1)
270 FOR I=1 TO N
280 FOR J=1 TO M
290 ?"ENTER THE FREQUENCY IN SET ";I;"CATEGORY";J;
300 INPUT O1(I,J)
310 NEXT J
320 NEXT I
330 FOR J=1 TO M:REM CALCULATE COLUMN TOTALS
340 FOR I=1 TO N
350 O1(N+1,J)=O1(N+1,J)+O1(I,J)
360 E1(N+1,J)=O1(N+1,J)
370 NEXT I
380 NEXT J
390 FOR I=1 TO N:REM CALCULATE ROW TOTALS
400 FOR J=1 TO M
410 o1(I,M+1)=O1(I,M+1)+O1(I,J)
420 E1(I,M+1)=O1(I,M+1)
430 NEXT J
440 NEXT I
450 FOR I=1 TO N
```

```basic
460 X=X+O1(I,M+1)
470 O1(N+1,M+1)=X:REM GRAND TOTAL
480 NEXT I
490 FOR I=1 TO N
500 FOR J=1 TO M
510 E1(I,J)=O1(N+1,J)*O1(I,M+1)/X:REM CALCULATE EXPECTED FREQUENCIES
520 NEXT J
530 NEXT I
540 ?:?:?:?:?:?:?:?:?:?
550 ? TAB(16) "SET 1":REM PRINT OUT CONTINGENCY TABLE
560 FOR I=1 TO M
570 ? TAB (10*I+10);I;
580 NEXT I
590 ? TAB(10*I+9) "TOTAL (O/E)";
600 ?
610 ? "SET 2"
620 FOR I=1 TO N+1
630 FOR J=1 TO M+1
640 IF J=1 AND I<>N+1 THEN ?"    ";I;"O";:REM OMIT "O" FROM "TOTAL" LINE
650 IF J=1 AND I=N+1 THEN ?TAB(7);"TOTAL (O/E)";
660 ? TAB(10+10*J);O1(I,J);
670 NEXT J
680 ?
690 FOR J=1 TO M+1
700 IF J=1 AND I<>N+1 THEN ?"   ";I;"E";
710 IF I<>N+1 THEN ?TAB(10+10*J);E1(I,J);
720 NEXT J
730 ?:?
740 NEXT I
750 ? TAB(30) "O: OBSERVED FREQUENCY"
760 ? TAB(30) "E:  EXPECTED FREQUENCY"
770 IF N=2 AND M=2 THEN Z=O1(3,3)*(ABS(O1(1,1)*O1(2,2)-O1(1,2)*O1(2,1))-O1(3,3)/2)^2/
(O1(3,1)*O1(3,2)*O1(2,3)*O1(1,3)):GOTO 830
780 FOR I=1 TO N
790 FOR J=1 TO M
800 Z=Z+(O1(I,J)-E1(I,J))^2/E1(I,J)
810 NEXT j
820 NEXT I
830 ?:?"CHI-SQUARE=";Z:?"C=";SQR(Z/(X+Z))
840 K=(N-1)*(M-1):?K;"DEGREE(S) OF FREEDOM": N=K:GOTO 1220
860 ?"ENTER THE NUMBER OF CATEGORIES IN SET 2(MAX=30)";
870 INPUT N:IF N>30 THEN ?"MUST BE <= 30":STOP
880 M=3
890 DIM O(N):DIM E(N)
900 FOR I=1 TO N
910 ?"ENTER THE OBSERVED FREQUENCY IN SET 2 CATEGORY";I
920 INPUT O(I)
930 ?"ENTER THE EXPECTED FREQUENCY IN SET 2 CATEGORY";I
940 INPUT E(I)
950 IF E(I)<5 THEN ?:?:?:?:?"OBSERVED FREQUENCY MUST BE 5 OR MORE":STOP
960 NEXT I
970 ?:?:?:?:?:?:?:?:?:?
980 ?"THE CONTINGENCY TABLE OF FREQUENCIES IS;"
990 ?
1000 ?"CATEGORY","OBSERVED","EXPECTED"
1010 ?
```

```
1020 FOR I=1 TO N
1030 ?I,O(I),E(I)
1040 NEXT I
1050 ?"-------------------------------------------------------------------"
1060 FOR I=1 TO N
1070 X=X+O(I)
1080 Y=Y+E(I)
1090 NEXT I
1100 ?"   TOTAL",X,Y
1110 FOR I=1 TO N
1120 Z=Z+(O(I)-E(I))^2/E(I)
1130 NEXT I
1140 ?:?:Y=INT(Z)
1150 Z=Z-INT(Z)
1160 Z=Z*10^M
1170 Z=INT(Z+.5)
1180 Z=Z/10^M
1190 Z=Z+Y
1200 ?"CHI-SQUARE=";Z:?"C=";SQR(Z/(X+Z))
1210 ? N-1;"DEGREE(S) OF FREEDOM":N=N-1
1220 ?:?"H(0):";
1230 IF Z=C(N) THEN ?"P=0.01":STOP
1240 IF Z>C(N) THEN ?"P<0.01":STOP
1250 IF Z=B(N) THEN ?"P=0.05":STOP
1260 IF Z>B(N) THEN ?"0.05>P>0.01":STOP
1270 IF Z=A(N) THEN ?"P=0.1":STOP
1280 IF Z<A(N) THEN ?"P>0.1":STOP
1290 IF Z>A(N) THEN ?"0.1>P>0.05":STOP
```

Print-out of the Fisher Exact test program

```
fishexact - Notepad
File  Edit  Format  View  Help
100 REM FISHER EXACT ONE-SIDED TEST FOR NOMINAL DATA
110 DIM O(3,3):DIM T(4,4):DIM O1(3,3)
120 FOR I=1 TO 2
130 FOR J=1 TO 2
140 ?"ENTER THE FREQUENCY IN CATEGORY";I;"SAMPLE";J;
150 INPUT O(I,J):O1(I,J)=O(I,J)
160 NEXT J
170 NEXT I
180 O1(3,1)=O(1,1):O1(3,2)=O(1,2):O1(3,3)=O(1,1):O1(1,3)=O(1,1):O1(2,3)=O(2,1)
190 T(4,1)=O(1,1)+O(2,1):T(4,2)=O(1,2)+O(2,2):T(4,3)=T(4,1):T(3,4)=O(1,1)+O(1,2):T(1,4)=T(3,4)
200 T(2,4)=O(2,1)+O(2,2)
210 FOR I=1 TO 3
220 FOR J=1 TO 3
230 O(I,J)=O1(I,J)
240 NEXT J:NEXT I
250 L=1:P=1
260 FOR I=1 TO 2
270 FOR J=1 TO 2
280 IF O1(1,1)<=O1(I,J) THEN 300
290 M=O1(1,1):O1(1,1)=O1(I,j):O1(I,J)=M:L=I:P=J
300 NEXT J
310 NEXT I
320 X=O(L,P)
330 N=T(1,4)+T(2,4)
340 ?"THE CONTINGENCY TABLE IS:":?:?
350 ?"SAMPLE 1","SAMPLE 2","TOTAL":?
360 ?"CATEGORY 1",O(1,1),O(1,2),T(1,4)
370 ?"CATEGORY 2",O(2,1),O(2,2),T(2,4):?
380 ?"TOTAL",T(4,1),T(4,2),N:?:?
390 K=N:GOSUB 570:NFACT=Y
400 FOR I=0 TO X
410 O(L,P)=X-I
420 O(L,P+1)=T(L,4)-O(L,P)
430 O(L+1,P)=T(4,P)-O(L,P)
440 O(L+1,P+1)=T(L+1,4)-O(L+1,P)
450 K=T(L,4):GOSUB 570:ABFACT=Y
460 K=T(L+1,4):GOSUB 570:CDFACT=Y
470 K=T(4,P):GOSUB 570:ACFACT=Y
480 K=T(4,P+1):GOSUB 570:BDFACT=Y
490 K=O(L,P):GOSUB 570:AFACT=Y
500 K=O(L,P+1):GOSUB 570:BFACT=Y
510 K=O(L+1,P):GOSUB 570:CFACT=Y
520 K=O(L+1,P+1):GOSUB 570:DFACT=Y
530 SUM=SUM + (ABFACT*CDFACT*ACFACT*BDFACT/NFACT)/(AFACT*BFACT*CFACT*DFACT)
540 NEXT I
550 ?:?"P=";SUM
560 STOP
```

```
570 Y=1
580 IF K=0 THEN 620
590 FOR J=1 TO K
600 Y=Y*J
610 NEXT J
620 RETURN
```

Print-out of the McNemar test program

```
MCNEMAR - Notepad
File  Edit  Format  View  Help
100 REM***CALCULATES CHI-SQUARE STATISTIC FOR TWO SAMPLE NOMINAL DATA
110 DIM A(30):DIM B(30):DIM C(30)
120 DATA
2.706,3.841,6.635,4.605,5.991,9.210,6.251,7.815,11.341,7.779,9.488,13.277,9.236,11.070,15.086
130 DATA
10.645,12.592,16.812,12.017,14.067,18.475,13.362,15.507,20.090,14.684,16.919,21.666,15.987,1
8.307,23.209
140 DATA
17.275,19.675,24.725,18.549,21.026,26.217,19.812,22.362,27.688,21.064,23.685,29.141,22.307,2
4.996,30.578
150 DATA
23.542,26.296,32.000,24.769,27.587,33.409,25.989,28.869,34.805,27.204,30.144,36.191,28.412,
31.410,37.566
160 DATA
29.615,32.671,38.932,30.813,33.924,40.289,32.007,35.172,41.638,33.196,36.415,42.980,34.382,3
7.652,44.314
170 DATA
35.563,38.885,45.642,36.741,40.113,46.963,37.916,41.337,48.278,39.087,42.557,49.588,40.256,
43.773,50.892
180 FOR I=1 TO 30
190 READ A(I),B(I),C(I)
200 NEXT I
210 REM MCNEMAR TEST FOR SIGNIFICANCE OF CHANGES: A 2-RELATED SAMPLE TEST
FOR NOMINAL DATA
220 ?"MAY BE USED WHERE SUBJECTS ACT AS THEIR OWN CONTROLS . e.g. FREQUENCY
OF SUBJECTS"
225 ?"  FAILING A TEST BEFORE TUITION WHO PASS  AFTER TUITION"
230 ?:?:?:? TAB(23),"AFTER"
240 ? TAB(15) "CATEGORY X" TAB(35) "CATEGORY Y"
250? TAB(10) "X" TAB(15) "A" TAB(35) "CATEGORY B"
260 ? "BEFORE":? TAB(10) "Y" TAB(15) "C" TAB(35) "D"
270 ?:?:?"ENTER FREQUENCY A";:INPUT A
280 ?"ENTER FREQUENCY B";:INPUT B
290 ?"ENTER FREQUENCY C";:INPUT C
300 ?"ENTER FREQUENCY D";:INPUT D
310 IF 0.5*(A+D)<5 THEN ?:?:?"EXPECTED FREQUENCY TOO SMALL: USE BINOMIAL
TEST":STOP
320 CHISQUARE=((A-D)*SGN(A-D)-1)^2/(A+D):Z=CHISQUARE
330 ?"CHI-SQUARE=";CHISQUARE;"1 DF":N=2
1220 ?:?"H(0):";
1230 IF Z=C(N-1) THEN ?"P=0.01":STOP
1240 IF Z>C(N-1) THEN ?"P<0.01":STOP
1250 IF Z=B(N-1) THEN ?"P=0.05":STOP
1260 IF Z>B(N-1) THEN ?"0.05>P>0.01":STOP
1270 IF Z=A(N-1) THEN ?"P=0.1":STOP
1280 IF Z<B(N-1) THEN ?"P>0.1":STOP
1290 IF Z>A(N-1) THEN ?"0.1>P>0.05":STOP
```

Print-out of the Chisquare k-sample test program

```
CHISQ - Notepad
File  Edit  Format  View  Help
100 REM***CONTINGENCY  TEST  OF THE SIGNIFANCE OF THE COORELATION BETWEEN
2 SETS OF CATEGORICAL (NOMINAL) DATA
110 DIM A(30):DIM B(30):DIM C(30)
120 DATA
2.706,3.841,6.635,4.605,5.991,9.210,6.251,7.815,11.341,7.779,9.488,13.277,9.236,11.070,15.086
130 DATA
10.645,12.592,16.812,12.017,14.067,18.475,13.362,15.507,20.090,14.684,16.919,21.666,15.987,1
8.307,23.209
140 DATA
17.275,19.675,24.725,18.549,21.026,26.217,19.812,22.362,27.688,21.064,23.685,29.141,22.307,2
4.996,30.578
150 DATA
23.542,26.296,32.000,24.769,27.587,33.409,25.989,28.869,34.805,27.204,30.144,36.191,28.412,
31.410,37.566
160 DATA
29.615,32.671,38.932,30.813,33.924,40.289,32.007,35.172,41.638,33.196,36.415,42.980,34.382,3
7.652,44.314
170 DATA
35.563,38.885,45.642,36.741,40.113,46.963,37.916,41.337,48.278,39.087,42.557,49.588,40.256,
43.773,50.892
180 FOR I=1 TO 30
190 READ A(I),B(I),C(I)
200 NEXT I
210 ?"ENTER THE NUMBER OF SAMPLES ";
220 INPUT M
230 REM
240 IF M=1 THEN 860
245 ?"ENTER THE NUMBER OF CATEGORIES";
250 INPUT N
260 DIM O1(N+1,M+1):DIM E1(N+1,M+1)
270 FOR I=1 TO N
280 FOR J=1 TO M
290 ?"ENTER THE FREQUENCY IN CATEGORY";I;"SAMPLE";J;
300 INPUT O1(I,J)
310 NEXT J
320 NEXT I
330 FOR J=1 TO M:REM CALCULATE COLUMN TOTALS
340 FOR I=1 TO N
350 O1(N+1,J)=O1(N+1,J)+O1(I,J)
360 E1(N+1,J)=O1(N+1,J)
370 NEXT I
380 NEXT J
390 FOR I=1 TO N:REM CALCULATE ROW TOTALS
400 FOR J=1 TO M
410 O1(I,M+1)=O1(I,M+1)+O1(I,J)
420 E1(I,M+1)=O1(I,M+1)
430 NEXT J
440 NEXT I
450 FOR I=1 TO N
460 X=X+O1(I,M+1)
470 O1(N+1,M+1)=X:REM GRAND TOTAL
480 NEXT I
```

```
490 FOR I=1 TO N
500 FOR J=1 TO M
510 E1(I,J)=O1(N+1,J)*O1(I,M+1)/X:REM CALCULATE EXPECTED FREQUENCIES
520 NEXT J
530 NEXT I
540 ?:?:?:?:?:?:?:?:?:?
550 ? TAB(16) "SAMPLE":REM PRINT OUT CONTINGENCY TABLE
560 FOR I=1 TO M
570 ? TAB (10*I+10);I;
580 NEXT I
590 ? TAB(10*I+9) "TOTAL (O/E)";
600 ?
610 ? "CATEGORY"
620 FOR I=1 TO N+1
630 FOR J=1 TO M+1
640 IF J=1 AND I<>N+1 THEN ?"    ";I;"O";:REM OMIT "O" FROM "TOTAL" LINE
650 IF J=1 AND I=N+1 THEN  ?TAB(7);"TOTAL (O/E)";
660 ? TAB(10+10*J);O1(I,J);
670 NEXT J
680 ?
690 FOR J=1 TO M+1
700 IF J=1 AND I<>N+1 THEN ?"    ";I;"E";
710 IF I<>N+1 THEN ?TAB(10+10*J);E1(I,J);
720 NEXT J
730 ?:?
740 NEXT I
750 ? TAB(30) "O: OBSERVED FREQUENCY"
760 ? TAB(30) "E:  EXPECTED FREQUENCY"
770 IF N=2 THEN Z=O1(3,3)*(ABS(O1(1,1)*O1(2,2)-O1(1,2)*O1(2,1))-O1(3,3)/2)^2/(O1(3,1)
*O1(3,2)*O1(2,3)*O1(1,3)):GOTO 830
780 FOR I=1 TO N
790 FOR J=1 TO M
800 Z=Z+(O1(I,J)-E1(I,J))^2/E1(I,J)
810 NEXT J
820 NEXT I
830 ?:?"CHI-SQUARE=";Z
840 N=(N-1)*(M-1):GOTO 1220:REM CALCULATE DEGREES OF FREEDOM
860 ?"ENTER THE NUMBER OF CATEGORIES (MAX=30)";
870 INPUT N:IF N>30 THEN ?"MUST BE <= 30":STOP
880 M=3
890 DIM O(N):DIM E(N)
900 FOR I=1 TO N
910 ?"ENTER THE OBSERVED FREQUENCY IN CATEGORY";I
920 INPUT O(I)
930 ?"ENTER THE EXPECTED FREQUENCY IN CATEGORY";I
940 INPUT E(I)
950 IF E(I)<5 THEN ?:?:?:?:?"OBSERVED FREQUENCY MUST BE 5 OR MORE":STOP
960 NEXT I
970 ?:?:?:?:?:?:?:?:?:?
980 ?"THE CONTINGENCY TABLE OF FREQUENCIES IS;"
990 ?
1000 ?"CATEGORY","OBSERVED","EXPECTED"
1010 ?
1020 FOR I=1 TO N
1030 ?I,O(I),E(I)
1040 NEXT I
1050 ?"--------------------------------------------------------------------------------"
1060 FOR I=1 TO N
1070 X=X+O(I)
1080 Y=Y+E(I)
```

```
1190 Z=Z+Y
1200 ?"CHI-SQUARE=";Z
1210 ? N-1;"DEGREE(S) OF FREEDOM"
1220 ?:?"H(0):";
1230 IF Z=C(N-1) THEN ?"P=0.01":STOP
1240 IF Z>C(N-1) THEN ?"P<0.01":STOP
1250 IF Z=B(N-1) THEN ?"P=0.05":STOP
1260 IF Z>B(N-1) THEN ?"0.05>P>0.01":STOP
1270 IF Z=A(N-1) THEN ?"P=0.1":STOP
1280 IF Z<B(N-1) THEN ?"P>0.1":STOP
1290 IF Z>A(N-1) THEN ?"0.1>P>0.05":STOP
```

Print-out of the Cochran Q k-sample test program

```
110 DIM B(30):DIM C(30):DIM D(30)
120 DATA
2.706,3.841,6.635,4.605,5.991,9.210,6.251,7.815,11.341,7.779,9.488,13.277,9.236,11.070,15.086
130 DATA
10.645,12.592,16.812,12.017,14.067,18.475,13.362,15.507,20.090,14.684,16.919,21.666,15.987,1
8.307,23.209
140 DATA
17.275,19.675,24.725,18.549,21.026,26.217,19.812,22.362,27.688,21.064,23.685,29.141,22.307,2
4.996,30.578
150 DATA
23.542,26.296,32.000,24.769,27.587,33.409,25.989,28.869,34.805,27.204,30.144,36.191,28.412,
31.410,37.566
160 DATA
29.615,32.671,38.932,30.813,33.924,40.289,32.007,35.172,41.638,33.196,36.415,42.980,34.382,3
7.652,44.314
170 DATA
35.563,38.885,45.642,36.741,40.113,46.963,37.916,41.337,48.278,39.087,42.557,49.588,40.256,
43.773,50.892
180 FOR I=1 TO 30
190 READ B(I),C(I),D(I)
200 NEXT I
290 ?"COCHRAN Q TEST FOR N RELATED SAMPLES OF DICHOTMOUS DATA"
291 ?"(pass/fail; 0/1; yes/no, etc.)"
292 ? "Each subject may be rated once on one characteristic in a matched subjects design"
294 ?"or a given subject may be rated on each characteristic in a repeated measures design"
300 ?"REPEATED MEASURES DESIGN PRESS [r]; MATCHED SUBJECTS DESIGN PRESS
[m]";
310 INPUT A$
320 ?"HOW MANY CHRACTERISTICS";
330 INPUT K
332 DIM G(K+1)
340 IF A$="r" THEN 1000
345?"HOW MANY SAMPLES";
350 INPUT N
360 DIM A(N+1,K+1):DIM L(N+1)
380 GOTO 2000
999 STOP
1000 ?"HOW MANY SUBJECTS";
1002 INPUT N
1003 DIM A(N+1,K+1):DIM L(N+1)
1005 FOR I=1 TO N:FOR J=1 TO K
1010 ?"ENTER [0] FOR FAIL/NO/ZERO, ETC.; ENTER [1] FOR PASS/YES/ONE, ETC. FOR
SUBJECT";I
1015 ?" ON CHARACTERISTIC";J;
1020 INPUT A(I,J)
1030 NEXT J:?:NEXT I
1100 FOR I=1 TO K: FOR J=1 TO N:G(I)=G(I)+A(J,I)
1110 NEXT J:NEXT I
1200 FOR I=1 TO N:FOR J=1 TO K:L(I)=L(I)+A(I,J)
1210 NEXT J:NEXT I
1220 FOR I=1 TO K:G=G+G(I):GSQ=GSQ+G(I)*G(I):NEXT I
1230 FOR I=1 TO N:L=L+L(I):LSQ=LSQ+L(I)*L(I):NEXT I
1240 Q=((K-1)*(K*GSQ-G*G))/(K*L-LSQ)
```

```
1241 IF K<>2 THEN 1250
1242 FOR I=1 TO N:IF A(I,1)<>A(I,2) THEN AD=AD+1
1243 NEXT I
1244 IF AD<10 THEN ?"USE MCNEMAR TEST":STOP
1250 ?"Q=";Q;" (";K-1;"DF)":N=K:Z=Q:GOTO 2220
1260 STOP
2000 FOR I=1 TO N:FOR J=1 TO K
2010 ?"ENTER [0] FOR FAIL/NO/ZERO, ETC. OR [1] FOR PASS/YES/ONE,ETC FOR SUBJECT
";J
2012 ? "SAMPLE";I;"CHARACTERISTIC";J;
2015 INPUT A(I,J)
2020 NEXT J:NEXT I
2030 GOTO 1100
2220 ?:?"H(0):";
2230 IF Z=D(N-1) THEN ?"P=0.01":STOP
2240 IF Z>D(N-1) THEN ?"P<0.01":STOP
2250 IF Z=C(N-1) THEN ?"P=0.05":STOP
2260 IF Z>C(N-1) THEN ?"0.05>P>0.01":STOP
2270 IF Z=B(N-1) THEN ?"P=0.1":STOP
2280 IF Z<C(N-1) THEN ?"P>0.1":STOP
2290 IF Z>B(N-1) THEN ?"0.1>P>0.05":STOP
```

Print-out of the Kolmogorov-Smirnov one sample test program

```
kolmog1s - Notepad
File   Edit   Format   View   Help
10 ?"Kolmogorov-Smirnov One Sample Test of Goodness of Fit to a user- chosen
distribition"
100 ?"DATA CAN BE RAW VALUES OR RANKS"
110 DIM CRITD(36,5)
120 DATA
.995,.975,.95,.925,.9,.929,.842,.776,.726,.684,.828,.708,.642,.597,.565,.733,.624,.564,.525,.494
130 DATA
.669,.565,.51,.474,.446,.618,.521,.47,.436,.41,.577,.486,.438,.405,.381,.543,.457,.411,.381,.358
140 DATA
.514,.432,.388,.36,.339,.49,.41,.368,.342,.322,.468,.391,.352,.326,.307,.45,.375,.338,.313,.295
150 DATA .433,.361,.325,.302,.284,.418,.349,.314,.292,.274,.404,.338,.304,.283,
.266,.392,.328,.295,.274,.258
160 DATA
.381,.318,.286,.266,.25,.371,.309,.278,.259,.244,.363,.301,.272,.252,.237,.356,.294,.264,.246,.23
1

170 DATA
.349,.289,.26,.241,.227,.342,.284,.254,.236,.223,.334,.28,.25,.23,.218,.327,.27,.245,.226,.214
180 DATA
.32,.27,.24,.22,.21,.314,.264,.236,.216,.206,.308,.258,.232,.212,.202,.302,.252,.228,.208,.198
190 DATA
.296,.246,.224,.204,.194,.29,.24,.22,.2,.19,.284,.238,.218,.198,.188,.278,.236,.216,.196,.186
200 DATA .272,.234,.214,.194,.184,.266,.232,.212,.192,.182,.27,.23,.21,.19,.18
210 DATA
.32,.27,.24,.22,.21,.32,.27,.24,.22,.21,.32,.27,.24,.22,.21,.32,.27,.24,.22,.21,.32,.27,.24,.22,.21
220 FOR I=1 TO 35:FOR J=1 TO 5
230 REM READ IN CRITICAL VALUES OF D
240 READ CRITD(I,J):NEXT j:NEXTi
250 ?"HOW MANY DATA";
260 INPUT N
270 DIM D(N+1):DIM COUNT (N+1)
280 DIM Y(N+1):DIM RANK(N+1)
290 DIM Z(N+1)
300 REM RANK THE DATA
310 FOR I=1 TO N
320 ?"ENTER DATUM";i;
330 INPUT Y(I)
340 NEXT I
350 FOR J=1 TO N-1
360 FOR I=J TO N-1
370 IF Y(J)<Y(I+1) THEN 410
380 K=Y(J)
390 Y(J)=Y(I+1)
400 Y(I+1)=K
410 NEXT I
420 NEXT J
540 GOSUB 930
550 ?:FOR I=1 TO N:?"ENTER THE CUMULATIVE P UNDER Ho OF DATUM VALUE";Y
(I);"OBSERVED CUMULATIVE P";I/N;"(";I;"/";N;")";
560 INPUT Z(I)
570 NEXT I
580 ?:?:?"DATUM","OBSERVED CUMULATIVE p","CUMULATIVE P UNDER Ho"
```

```
590 FOR I=1 TO N
600 ?Y(I),I/N,,Z(I)
611 IF I/29-INT(I/29)=0 THEN ?"MORE (NOTE DOWN MAX. DEVIATION SO FAR BEFORE
PRESSING ANY KEY";:INPUT A$
612 NEXT I
620 ?:?"ENTER MAX. DEVIANCE BY INSPECTION OF ABOVE TABLE";
630 INPUT DMAX
640 ?:?:? "2-SIDED ";
650 IF N>35 THEN GOSUB 860:GOTO700
660 FOR J=1 TO 5
670 IF DMAX>CRITd(N,J) THEN GOSUB 800:GOTO 700
680 NEXT J
690 ?"P>.2"
700 STOP
800 X=(DMAX-CRITD(N,J))/(CRITD(N,J-1)-CRITD(N,J))
810 ON J GOTO 820,830,840,840,840
820 ?"P<.01":GOTO 850
830 ?"P=";.05-.04*X:GOTO 850
840 ?"P=";.2-.05*(5-J)-.05*X:GOTO 850
850 RETURN
860 IF DMAX>1.63/SQR(N) THEN ?"P<.01":RETURN
870 IF DMAX>1.36/SQR(N) THEN ?".01<P<.05":RETURN
880 IF DMAX>1.22/SQR(N) THEN ?".05<P<.1":RETURN
890 IF DMAX>1.14/SQR(N) THEN ?".1<P<.15":RETURN
900 IF DMAX>1.07/SQR(N) THEN ?".15<P<.2":RETURN
910 ?"P..2":RETURN
920 REM FORM CUMULATIVE RANKINGS
930 FOR I=1 TO N
940 FOR J=1 TO N
950 IF Y(I)=Y(J) THEN COUNT(I)=COUNT(I)+1
960 NEXT J:NEXT I
970 FOR I=1 TO N
980 FOR M=1 TO COUNT(I)
990 RANK(I+M-1)=RANK(I-1)+COUNT(I)
1000 NEXT M
1010 I=I+COUNT(I)-1
1020 NEXT I
1030 RETURN
```

Print-out of the one -sample runs test program

```
RUNSTEST1S - Notepad
File  Edit  Format  View  Help
10 REM RUNS TEST OF RANDOMNESS IN THE ORDER OF DATA IN ONE SAMPLE
20 REM THE DATA ARE DICHOTOMIZED W.R.T. SOME CRITERION E.G. EXCEED/DO NOT
EXCEED SOME VALUE
22 GOSUB 1000:DIM CRITR(40,20)
24 FOR I=1 TO 38:FOR J=1 TO 19:READ CRITR(I,J):NEXT J:NEXT I
30 ?"ENTER THE NUMBER OF DATA";
40 INPUT N
50 DIM X$(N+1)
60 FOR I=1 TO N
70 ?"ENTER 1 OR 0 FOR DATUM";I;
80 INPUT X$(I)
90 IF X$(I)<>"0" AND X$(I)<>"1" THEN ?"RE-DO":GOTO 70
91 IF X$(I)="1" THEN N1=N1+1:GOTO 100
92 N2=N2+1
100 NEXT I
110 R=1
120 FOR I=1 TO N-1
130 IF X$(I)=X$(I+1) THEN 150
140 R=R+1
150 NEXT I
200 ?:?:?"R=";R;:?"  N1=";N1;:?"  N2=";N2:IF N1>20 OR N2>20 THEN 300
210 IF R<=CRITR(N1-1,N2-1) THEN ?"P<=0.05":GOTO 240
220 IF R>=CRITR(N1+18,N2-1) OR R>=CRITR(N2+18,N1-1) THEN ?"P<=0.05":GOTO 240
230 ?"P>0.05. ORDERING OF DATA IS RANDOM"
240 STOP
300 Z=(R-(2*N1*N2/(N1+N2)+1))/SQR((2*N1*N2*(2*N1*N2-N1-N2)/((N1+N2)^2*(N1+N2-
1))))
310 ?:?"Z=" ;Z:STOP
1000 DATA 0,0,0,0,0,0,0,0,0,0,2,2,2,2,2,2,2,2,0,0,0,0,2,2,2,2,2,2,2,2,3,3,3,3,3
1010 DATA 0,0,0,2,2,2,3,3,3,3,3,3,3,3,4,4,4,4,4,0,0,2,2,3,3,3,3,3,4,4,4,4,4,4,5,5,5
1020 DATA 0,2,2,3,3,3,3,4,4,4,4,5,5,5,5,5,5,6,6,0,2,2,3,3,3,4,4,5,5,5,5,5,6,6,6,6,6,6
1030 DATA 0,2,3,3,3,4,4,5,5,5,6,6,6,6,7,7,7,7,0,0,2,3,3,4,4,5,5,5,6,6,6,7,7,7,7,8,8,8
1040 DATA 0,2,3,3,4,5,5,5,6,6,7,7,7,7,8,8,8,8,9,0,2,3,4,4,5,5,6,6,7,7,7,8,8,8,9,9,9,9
1060 DATA 2,2,3,4,4,5,6,6,7,7,7,8,8,8,9,9,9,10,10,2,2,3,4,5,5,6,6,7,7,8,8,9,9,9,10,10,10,10
1070 DATA 2,2,3,4,5,5,6,7,7,8,8,9,9,9,10,10,10,11,11,2,3,3,4,5,6,6,7,7,8,8,9,9,10,10,10,11,11,11,12
1080 DATA
2,3,4,4,5,6,6,7,8,8,9,9,10,10,11,11,11,12,12,2,3,4,4,5,6,7,7,8,9,9,10,10,11,11,11,12,12,13
1090 DATA
2,3,4,5,5,6,7,8,8,9,9,10,10,11,11,12,12,13,13,2,3,4,5,6,6,7,8,8,9,10,10,11,11,12,12,13,13,13
1100 DATA 2,3,4,5,6,6,7,8,9,9,10,10,11,12,12,13,13,14
1200 DATA 0,0,0,0,0,0,0,0,0,0,0,0,0,0,0,0,0,0,0,0,0,0,0,0,0,0,0,0,0,0,0,0,0,0,0,0,0,0
1210 DATA 0,0,0,9,9,0,0,0,0,0,0,0,0,0,0,0,0,0,0,0,9,10,10,11,11,0,0,0,0,0,0,0,0,0,0,0,0
1220 DATA
0,0,9,10,11,12,12,13,13,13,13,0,0,0,0,0,0,0,0,0,11,12,13,13,14,14,14,14,15,15,15,0,0,0,0
1230 DATA
0,0,0,11,12,13,14,14,15,15,16,16,16,16,17,17,17,17,0,0,0,0,0,13,14,14,15,16,16,16,17,17,18,18,18
,18,18,18
1240 DATA
0,0,0,0,13,14,15,16,16,17,17,18,18,18,19,19,19,20,20,0,0,0,0,13,14,15,16,17,17,18,19,19,19,20,20
,20,21,21
1250 DATA
0,0,0,0,13,14,16,16,17,18,19,19,20,20,21,21,21,22,22,0,0,0,0,0,15,16,17,18,19,19,20,20,21,21,22,
22,23,23
```

```
1260 DATA
0,0,0,0,0,0,15,16,17,18,19,20,20,21,22,22,23,23,23,24,0,0,0,0,0,15,16,18,18,19,20,21,22,22,23,23,
24,24,25
1270 DATA
0,0,0,0,0,0,17,18,19,20,21,21,22,23,23,24,25,25,25,0,0,0,0,0,0,17,18,19,20,21,22,23,23,24,25,25
,26,26
1280 DATA
0,0,0,0,0,0,17,18,19,20,21,22,23,24,25,25,26,26,27,0,0,0,0,0,0,17,18,20,21,22,23,23,24,25,26,2
6,27,27
1290 DATA 0,0,0,0,0,0,17,18,20,21,22,23,24,25,25,26,27,27,28
1300 RETURN
```

Print-out of the two-sample Spearman correlation test program

```
SPEARMAN - Notepad
File  Edit  Format  View  Help
10 REM SPEARMAN CORRELATION TEST FOR RANKED DATA
100 DATA 1.701,2.048,2.763,1.699,2.043,2.756,1.697,2.042,2.750
110 DATA 1.684,2.021,2.704,1.671,2.000,2.660,1.658,1.980,2.617
120 DATA 1.645,1.960,2.576
130 DIM O(7):DIM P(7):DIM Q(7)
140 FOR I=1 TO 7:READ I(I),P(I),Q(I):NEXT I
150 DATA 0,1,2,0,.9,.1,0,.829,.943
160 DATA .714,.786,.929,.643,.738,.881,.600,.683,.833,.564,.648,.794
170 DATA .564,.648,.794,.506,.591,.777,.506,.591,.777,.456,.544,.715,.456,.544,.715
180 DATA .425,.506,.665,.425,.506,.665,.399,.475,.625,.399,.475,.625
190 DATA .377,.450,.591,.377,.450,.591,.359,.428,.562,.359,.428,.562
200 DATA .343,.409,.537,.343,.409,.537,.329,.392,.515,.329,.392,.515
210 DATA .317,.377,.496,.317,.377,.496,.306,.364,.478,.306,.364,.478
220 DIM E(30):DIM F(30):DIM G(30)
230 FOR I=4 TO 30:READ E(I),F(I),G(I):NEXT I

240 ?"ENTER THE NUMBER OF PAIRS OF DATA"
250 INPUT N:IF N<4 THEN ?"AT LEAST 4 PAIRS":STOP
260 DIM X(N+1):DIMY(N+1)
270 FOR I=1 TO N
280 ?"ENTER SAMPLE 1 DATUM";i;
290 INPUT Y(I)
300 ?"ENTER SAMPLE 2 DATUM";I;
310 INPUT X(I)
320 NEXT I
325 REM RANK THE DATA IN EACH SAMPLE
330 FOR J=1 TO N-1
340 FOR I=J TO N-1
350 IF X(J)<X(I+1) THEN 390
360 K=X(J):M=Y(J)
370 X(J)=X(I+1):Y(J)=Y(I+1)
380 X(I+1)=K:Y(I+1)=M
390 NEXT I
400 NEXT J
410 ?:?
420 DIM B(N+1):K=1
430 FOR J=1 TO N-1
440 FOR I=J TO N-1
450 IF X(J)=X(I+1) THEN B(K)=B(K)+1
460 NEXT I:J=J+B(K):K=K+1
470 NEXT J
480 FOR I=1 TO K:B(I)=B(I)+1:NEXT I
490 DIM R(N+1)
500 J=1
510 FOR I=1 TO K
520 IF B(I)>1 THEN 570
530 R(J)=J
540 J=J+1
550 NEXT I
560 GOTO 620
570 M=J
580 FOR J=M TO M+B(I)-1
590 R(J)=(M*B(I)+(B(I)*B(I)-B(I))/2)/B(I)
600 NEXT J
```

```
610 GOTO 550
620 FOR J=1 TO N-1
630 FOR I=J TO N-1
640 IF Y(J)<Y(I+1) THEN 680
650 K=Y(J):M=R(J):L=X(J)
660 Y(J)=Y(I+1):R(J)=R(I+1):X(J)=X(I+1)
670 Y(I+1)=K:R(I+1)=M:X(I+1)=L
680 NEXT I
690 NEXT J
700 DIM C(N+1):DIM U(N+1):K=1
710 FOR J=1 TO N-1
720 FOR I=J TO N-1
730 IF Y(J)=Y(I+1) THEN C(K)=C(K)+1
740 NEXT I:U(K)=Y(J):J=J+C(K):K=K+1
750 NEXT J:U(K)=Y(K)
760 FOR I=1 TO K:C(I)=C(I)+1:NEXT I
770 DIM S(N+1)
780 J=1
790 FOR I=1 TO K
800 IF C(I)>1 THEN 880
810 S(J)=J
820 J=J+1
830 NEXT I
840 ?"RANKED DATA PAIRS:":?:?
850 ?"SAMPLE 1","RANK","SAMPLE 2","RANK"
860 ?:FOR I=1 TO N:IF I/29-INT(I/29)=0 THEN ? "MORE>>";:INPUT A$
865 ?Y(I),S(I),X(I),R(I):NEXT I
870 GOTO 930
880 M=J
890 FOR J=M TO M+C(I)-1
        ...................................
910 NEXT J
920 GOTO 830
930 FOR I=1 TO N:DSQ=DSQ+(S(I)-R(I))*(S(I)-R(I)):NEXT I
940 DSQ=1-(6*DSQ/(N*(N*N-1)))
950 ?:?" SPEARMAN Rs (UNCOORECTED FOR TIES)=";DSQ
960 ?"CORRECTION FOR TIES:"
965 ?"USE PEARSON CORRELATION OR"
970 ?"ENTER SIGMA Tx";
980 INPUT TX
990 ?"ENTER SIGMA Ty";
1000 INPUT TY
1010 X=DSQ*((N^3-N)/6)-TX-TY
1020 Y=((N^3-N)/12-TX)*((N^3-N)/12-TY)
1030 Y=2*SQR(Y):DSQ=X/Y
1040 ?"SPEARMAN Rs (CORRECTED FOR TIES)"; DSQ
1050 DSQ=ABS(DSQ):?
1060 IF N>30 THEN 2090
1070 ?
1080 IF N>=4 AND N<=6 THEN 2030
2000 IF DSQ<E(N) THEN ?"P>0.1"
2010 IF DSQ=E(N) THEN ?"P=0.1"
2020 IF DSQ>E(N) AND DSQ<F(N) THEN ?"0.1>P>0.05"
2030 IF DSQ=F(N) THEN ?"P=0.05"
2040 IF DSQ>F(N) AND DSQ<G(N) THEN ?"0.05>P>0.01"
2050 IF DSQ=G(N) THEN ?"P=0.01"
2060 IF DSQ>g(N) THEN ?"P<0.01"
2070 IF N>=4 AND N<=6 AND DSQ<0.829 THEN ?"P>0.05"
2080 STOP
2090 T=DSQ*SQR((N-2)/(1-DSQ^2))
2100 ?"t=",T;N-2;"DEGREES OF FREEDOM"
2110 IF N<32 THEN N=N-30
```

```
2120 IF N>=33 AND N<40 THEN N=3
2130 IF N>=40 AND N<60 THEN N=4
2140 IF N>=60 AND N<120 THEN N=5
2150 IF N>=120 AND N<240 THEN N=6
2160 IF N>240 THEN N=7
2170 IF T>O(N) THEN ?"P>0.1"
2180 IF T=O(N) THEN ?"P=0.1"
2190 IF T>O(N) AND T<P(N) THEN ?"0.1>P>0.05"
2200 IF T=P(N) THEN ?"P=0.05"
2210 IF T>P(N) AND T<Q(N) THEN ?"0.05>P>0.01"
2220 IF T=Q(N) THEN ?"P=0.01"
2230 IF T>Q(N) THEN ?"P<0.01"
```

155

Print-out of the 2-sample Median test program

```
5 REM MEDIAN TEST FOR TWO INDEPENDENT SAMPLES WITH DATA IN AT LEAST AN
ORDINAL SCALE
6 GOSUB 1000
10 ?"HOW MANY DATA IN THE LARGER SAMPLE (OR FIRST SAMPLE IF EQUAL)";
20 INPUT N
30 ?"HOW MANY DATA IN THE SMALLER SAMPLE (OR SECOND SAMPLE IF EQUAL)";
40 INPUT M
50 DIM A(N):DIM B(N)
60 DIM Z(N+M+1)
70 ?"ENTER EACH DATUM IN THE FIRST SAMPLE: BEGIN AFTER THE PROMPT"
80 FOR I=1 TO N:INPUT A(I):Z(I)=A(I):NEXT I
90 ?"ENTER EACH DATUM IN THE SECOND SAMPLE: BEGIN AFTER THE PROMPT"
100 FOR I=1 TO M:INPUT B(I):Z(I+N)=B(I):NEXT I
110 X=N+M
120 FOR I=1 TO X-1
130 FOR J=I TO X-1
140 IF Z(I)>Z(J+1) THEN Y=Z(I):Z(I)=Z(J+1):Z(J+1)=Y
150 NEXT J
160 NEXT I
170 ?"THE RANKED DATA FOR THE SAMPLES COMBINED IS:":FOR I=1 TO M+N:? Z
(I);:NEXT I
180 ?:?:?
330 IF INT(X/2)-X/2<0 THEN MED=Z(INT(X/2+1)):?"MEDIAN=";MED:GOTO 500
340 MED=(Z((X-1)/2)+Z((X+1)/2))/2:?"MEDIAN=";MED
500 FOR I=1 TO N:IF A(I)>=MED THEN A=A+1
510 NEXT I
600 FOR I=1 TO M:IF B(I)>=MED THEN B=B+1
610 NEXT I
700 ?:?:? TAB(20);"SAMPLE 1";TAB(35);"SAMPLE 2"
710 ?"ABOVE G/MEDIAN";TAB (20);A;TAB (35);B
720 ?"BELOW G/MEDIAN";TAB (20);N-A;TAB (35);M-B
800 IF ((A+B)*N/X<5 OR (A+B)*M/X<5 OR (X-(A+B))*N/X<5 OR (X-(A+B))*M/X<5) THEN
?"USE FISHER EXACT TEST":STOP
810 IF X<20 THEN ?"USE FISHER EXACT TEST":STOP
820 CHISQ=X*(ABS(A*(M-B)-B*(N-A))-X/2)^2/((A+B)*(N-A+M-B)*N*M)
830 ?"CHI-SQUARE=";CHISQ;" (1 DEGREE OF FREEDOM)":GOTO 1220
1000 REM***LOOK-UP TABLE
1110 DIM C(30):DIM D(30):DIM E(30)
1120 DATA
2.706,3.841,6.635,4.605,5.991,9.210,6.251,7.815,11.341,7.779,9.488,13.277,9.236,11.070,15.086
1130 DATA
10.645,12.592,16.812,12.017,14.067,18.475,13.362,15.507,20.090,14.684,16.919,21.666,15.987,
18.307,23.209
1140 DATA
17.275,19.675,24.725,18.549,21.026,26.217,19.812,22.362,27.688,21.064,23.685,29.141,22.307,
24.996,30.578
1150 DATA
23.542,26.296,32.000,24.769,27.587,33.409,25.989,28.869,34.805,27.204,30.144,36.191,28.41
2,31.410,37.566
1160 DATA
29.615,32.671,38.932,30.813,33.924,40.289,32.007,35.172,41.638,33.196,36.415,42.980,34.382,
37.652,44.314
1170 DATA
35.563,38.885,45.642,36.741,40.113,46.963,37.916,41.337,48.278,39.087,42.557,49.588,40.256,
43.773,50.892
1180 FOR I=1 TO 30
```

```
1190 READ C(I),D(I),E(I)
1200 NEXT I:RETURN
1220 ?:?"H(0):";
1230 IF CHISQ=E(1) THEN ?"P=0.01":STOP
1240 IF CHISQ>E(1) THEN ?"P<0.01":STOP
1250 IF CHISQ=D(1) THEN ?"P=0.05":STOP
1260 IF CHISQ>D(1) THEN ?"0.05>P>0.01":STOP
1270 IF CHISQ=C(1) THEN ?"P=0.1":STOP
1280 IF CHISQ<D(1) THEN ?"P>0.1":STOP
1290 IF CHISQ>C(1) THEN ?"0.1>P>0.05":STOP
```

Print-out of the 2-sample Mann-Whitney 'U' test program

```
MWUTEST - Notepad
File   Edit   Format   View   Help
5 REM MANN-WHITNEY 'U' TEST FOR 2 INDEPENDENT SAMPLES AND RANKED DATA
10 ?"HOW MANY DATA IN SAMPLE 1?";
20 INPUT M
30 ?"HOW MANY DATA IN SAMPLE 2?";
40 INPUT L
50 N=M+L
60 DIM RX(N+1):DIM RY(N+1)
70 DIM X(N+1):DIM Y(N+1):DIM XX(N+1)
80 GOSUB 570
90 FOR I=1 TO M
100 ?"ENTER DATUM";i;"SAMPLE 1";
110 INPUT X(I):XX(I)=X(I)
120 NEXT I
130 FOR I= M+1 TO N
140 ?"ENTER DATUM";I-M;"SAMPLE 2";
150 INPUT X(I):Y(I-M)=X(I)
160 NEXT I
170 REM ORDER THE DATA
180 FOR J=1 TO N-1
190 FOR I=J TO N-1
200 IF X(J)<X(I+1) THEN 240
210 K=X(J)
220 X(J)=X(I+1)
230 X(I+1)=K
240 NEXT I
250 NEXT J
260 ?:?
270 DIM B(N+1):K=1
280 REM FREQUENCY-1 OF GIVEN DATUM X(I) IS IN B(I)
290 FOR J=1 TO N-1
300 FOR I=J TO N-1
310 IF X(J)=X(I+1) THEN B(K)=B(K)+1
320 NEXT I:J=J+B(K):K=K+1
330 NEXT J
340 REM
350 FOR I=1 TO K:B(I)=B(I)+1:NEXT I
360 REM RANK SDATA IN X(I) AND STORE RANKS IN R(I)
370 DIM R(N+1)
380 J=1
390 FOR I=1 TO K
400 IF B(I)>1 THEN 450
410 R(J)=J
420 J=J+1
430 NEXT I
440 GOTO 500
450 X=J
460 FOR J=X TO X+B(I)-1
470 R(J)=(X*B(I)+(B(I)^2-B(I))/2)/B(I)
480 NEXT J
490 GOTO 430
500 REM
510 FOR I=1 TO N:FOR J=1 TO N
520 IF X(I)=XX(J) THEN RX(J)=R(I)
530 IF X(I)=Y(J) THEN RY(J)=R(I)
540 NEXT J:NEXT I
```

```
540 NEXT J:NEXT I
541 FOR I=1 TO M:U1=U1+RX(I):NEXT I
542 FOR I=1 TO L:U2=U2+RY(I):NEXT I
543 U1=M*L+(M*(M+1)/2)-U1
544 U2=M*L+(L*(L+1)/2)-U2
545 U1=ABS(U1):U2=ABS(U2): ?"U=";:IF U1>U2 THEN u=U2:?U:GOTO 1000
566 U=U1:?U:GOTO 1000
570 FOR I=1 TO N:X(I)=999.999:XX(I)=X(I):Y(I)=X(I):NEXT I
580 RETURN
1000 IF M<8 OR L<8 THEN ?"USE TABLES TO FIND  SIGNIFICANCE OF U":STOP
1010 Z=(U-M*L/2)/SQR((M*L*(M+L+1)/12)):?"Z=";Z
1015 Z=ABS(Z):IF Z<1.65 THEN ?"P>0.1":STOP
1017 IF Z>=1.65 AND Z<1.96 THEN ?"0.1>P>0.05":STOP
1020 IF Z<1.96 THEN ?"P>0.05":STOP
1030 IF Z>=1.96 AND Z<2.33 THEN ?"0.05>p>0.01":STOP
1040 IF Z>=2.33 THEN ? "P<0.01"
```

Print-out of the 2-sample Sign test program

```
SIGNTEST - Notepad                                              [_][□][X]
File   Edit   Format   View   Help
10 REM SIGN TEST FOR MATCHED PAIRS OF DATA, DATUM IN EACH PAIR RANKABLE
20 ?"ENTER THE NUMBER OF DATA PER SAMPLE";
30 INPUT N
35 ?:DIM X(N,2)
40 FOR I=1 TO N
50 ?"ENTER DATUM";I;"SAMPLE 1";
55 INPUT X(I,1)
60 ?"ENTER DATUM";I;"SAMPLE 2";
65 INPUT X(I,2)
70 ?:NEXT I
100 FOR I=1 TO N
110 IF SGN(X(I,1)-X(I,2))=1 THEN P=P+1
120 IF SGN(X(I,1)-X(I,2))=-1 THEN NEG=NEG+1
130 NEXT I
200 ?:?:?"(SAMPLE1-SAMPLE2)+ OBSERVED (EXPECTED)";TAB(30);"(SAMPLE1-
SAMPLE2)- OBSERVED (EXPECTED)"
210 ?:? P;"(";0.5*(NEG+P);")";TAB(30);NEG;"(";0.5*(NEG+P);")"
300 IF NEG+P<25 THEN GOSUB 2000:STOP
310 IF P>.5*(NEG+P) THEN ?"Z=";((P+.5)-.5*(NEG+P))/(.5*SQR(NEG+P)):GOSUB
1000:STOP
320 IF P<.5*(NEG+P) THEN ?"Z=";((P+.5)-.5*(NEG+P))/(.5*SQR(NEG+P)):GOSUB
1000:STOP
330 ?"Z=";(P-.5*(P+NEG))/(SQR(NEG+P))
1000 REM
1015 Z=ABS(Z):IF Z<1.65 THEN ?"P>0.1":STOP
1017 IF Z>=1.65 AND Z<1.96 THEN ?"0.1>P>0.05":STOP
1020 IF Z<1.96 THEN ?"P>0.05":STOP
1030 IF Z>=1.96 AND Z<2.33 THEN ?"0.05>p>0.01":STOP
1040 IF Z>=2.33 THEN ? "P<0.01"
1050 STOP
2000 N=NEG+P:K=N:P=0.5:GOSUB 2100:NFACT=Y
2025 GOSUB 2030
2027 GOTO 2080
2030 FOR I=0 TO NEG
2040 K=I:GOSUB 2100:XFACT=Y
2050 K=N-I:GOSUB 2100:NXFACT=Y
2060 SUM=SUM+(NFACT/(XFACT*NXFACT))*P^I*(1-P)^(N-I)
2070 NEXT I
2075 RETURN
2080 IF SUM>0.5 THEN SUM=1-SUM
2085 ? "P=";SUM
2090 STOP
2100 Y=1
2110 IF K=0 THEN 2150
2120 FOR J=1 TO K
2130 Y=Y*J
2140 NEXT J
2150 RETURN
```

Print-out of the 2-sample Wilcoxon signed ranks test program

```
5 ?"WILCOXON SIGNED RANKS TEST FOR MATCHED SAMPLES"
7 GOSUB 1000
10 ?"HOW MANY DATA IN EACH SAMPLE?";
20 INPUT N:Q=N
30 DIM X(N+1):DIM A(N+1):DIM B(N+1):DIM C(N+1)
31 DIM R(N+1)
40 FOR I=1 TO N
41 IF I>N THEN 100
43 L=L+1
50 ?"ENTER DATUM";L;"SAMPLE 1";
60 INPUT A(I)
70 ?"ENTER DATUM";L;"SAMPLE 2";
80 INPUT C(I)
82 IF A(I)-C(I)=0 THEN I=I-1:N=N-1
90 ?:NEXT I
100 FOR I=1 TO N:X(I)=A(I)-C(I):NEXT I
110 REM ORDER DATA
120 FOR J=1 TO N-1
130 FOR I=J TO N-1
140 IF ABS(X(J))<ABS(X(I+1)) THEN 180
150 K=X(J)
160 X(J)=X(I+1)
170 X(I+1)=K
180 NEXT I
190 NEXT J
200 ?:?
210 K=1
220 REM (FREQUENCY-1) OF GIVEN DATUM X(I) IN B(I)
230 FOR J=1 TO N-1
240 FOR I=J TO N-1
250 IF ABS(X(J))=ABS(X(I+1)) THEN B(K)=B(K)+1
260 NEXT I:J=J+B(K):K=K+1
270 NEXT J
280 REM FREQUENCY OF GIVEN DATUM X(I) IN B(I)
290 FOR I=1 TO K:B(I)=B(I)+1:NEXT I
300 REM RANK DATA IN X(I) AND STORE RANKS IN R(I)
320 J=1
330 FOR I=1 TO K
340 IF B(I)>1 THEN 390
350 R(J)=J
360 J=J+1
370 NEXT I
380 GOTO 440
390 M=J
400 FOR J=M TO M+B(I)-1
410 R(J)=(M*B(I)+(B(I)^2-B(I))/2)/B(I)
420 NEXT J
430 GOTO 370
440 ?:?:?"DIFFERENCE",,"RANK"
450 FOR I=1 TO N
460 ?X(I),,R(I)
465 IF SGN(X(I))=1 THEN RPOS=RPOS+R(I):P=P+1:GOTO 470
466 RNEG=RNEG+R(I)
470 NEXT I
```

```
471 ?:?
480 IF P>N-P THEN T=RNEG:GOTO 500
490 T=RPOS
500 ?"T=";T
510 ?"N=";N
515 IF Q<=25 THEN 2000
520 N=Q:?:?"Z=";(T-(N*(N+1)/4))/SQR(N*(N+1)*(2*N+1)/24)
530?"2-SIDED:": Z=ABS(Z):IF Z=1.96 THEN ?"P=0.05":STOP
540 IF Z>=1.96 AND Z<2.33 THEN ?"0.05>P>.01":STOP
550 IF Z>=2.33 THEN ?"P<0.01":STOP
560 IF Z<1.96 THEN ?"P>0.05":STOP
1000 DATA 0,-1,-1,2,0,-1,4,2,0,6,3,2,8,5,3,11,7,5,14,10,7,17,13,10,21,16,13,25,20,16
1010 DATA
30,24,20,35,28,23,40,33,28,46,38,32,52,43,38,59,49,43,66,56,49,73,62,55,81,69,61,89,77,68
1020 DIM W(26,4)
1030 FOR I= 6 TO 25:FOR j=1 TO 3:READ W(I,j):NEXT J:NEXT I
1040 RETURN
2000 ?"2-SIDED:":IF T>W(N,1) THEN ?"P>0.05":STOP
2005 IF T=W(N,1) THEN ?"P=0.05":STOP
2010 IF T>W(N,3) THEN ?"0.05>P>0.01":STOP
2020 IF T<=W(N,3) THEN ?"p<0.01":STOP
```

Print-out of the Concordance test program

```
concordance - Notepad
File  Edit  Format  View  Help

10 GOSUB 1000:GOSUB 3000
100 REM KENDALL'S CONCORDANCE TEST FOR K SAMPLES AND N CHARACTERISTICS
102 REM WITH RANKED DATA
110 ?"ENTER THE NUMBER OF SAMPLES";
120 INPUT M
130 ?"ENTER THE NUMBER OF CHARACTERISTICS";
140 INPUT N
150 DIM SUM(N+1)
160 DIM B(M+1,N+1):DIM R(M+1,N+1)
170 DIM RANK (M+1,N+1):DIM Y(M+1,N+1)
180 DIM X(M+1,N+1)
190 DIM T(M+1)
200 FOR I=1 TO M
210 FOR J=1 TO N
220 ?"ENTER DATUM FOR SAMPLE";I;"CHARACTERISTIC"J;
230 INPUT X(I,J):Y(I,J)=X(I,J):NEXT J
240 NEXT I
250 FOR K=1 TO M:X=1:GOSUB 430:NEXT K
260 GOSUB 740
270 FOR I=1 TO N
280 FOR J=1 TO M
290 SUM(I)=SUM(I)+RANK(J,I)
300 NEXT J:NEXT I
310 FOR I=1 TO N:SUM=SUM+SUM(I):NEXT I
320 FOR I=1 TO N:S=S+(SUM(I)-SUM/N)^2:NEXT I
330 FOR I=1 TO M:FOR J=1 TO N
340 IF B(I,J)>1 THEN T(I)=T(I)+B(I,J)^3-B(I,J)
350 NEXT J:NEXT I
```

```
360 FOR I=1 TO M:T=T+T(I):NEXT I
370 W=S/((1/12)*M^2*(N^3-N)-M*T/12)
380 ?"W=";W;"CORRECTED FOR TIES"
390 ?"AVERAGE SPEARMAN Rs FOR EACH PAIR OF SAMPLES =";(M*W-1)/(M-1)
400 IF N<=7 THEN GOTO 2000
410 CHISQ=M*(N-1)*W:?"CHI-SQUARE=";CHISQ;"WITH";N-1;"DEGREES OF FREEDOM"
420 GOTO 4000
430 REM ORDER DATA
440 FOR J=1 TO N-1
450 FOR I=J TO N-1
460 IF X(K,J)>X(K,I+1) THEN 500
470 Y=X(K,J)
480 X(K,J)=X(K,I+1)
490 X(K,I+1)=Y
500 NEXT I
510 NEXT J
520 ?:?
530 REM FREQUENCY OF GIVEN DATUM X(I) IN B(I)
540 FOR J=1 TO N-1
550 FOR I=J TO N-1
560 IF X(K,J)=X(K,I+1) THEN B(K,X)=B(K,X)+1
570 NEXT I:J=J+B(K,X):X=X+1
580 NEXT J
```

```
590 REM (FREQUENCY -1) OF GIVEN DATUM X(I) IN  B(I)
600 FOR I=1 TO X:B(K,I)=B(K,I)+1:NEXT I
610 REM RANK DATA IN X(I) AND STORE RANKS IN R(I)
620 J=1
630 FOR I=1 TO X
640 IF B(K,I)>1 THEN 690
650 R(K,J)=J
660 J=J+1
670 NEXT I
680 RETURN
690 L=J
700 FOR J=L TO L+B(K,I)-1
710 R(K,J)=(L*B(K,I)+(B(K,I)^2-B(K,I))/2)/B(K,I)
720 NEXT J
730 GOTO 670
740 FOR K=1 TO M
750 FOR I=1 TO N
760 FOR J=1 TO N
770 IF Y(K,I)=X(K,J) THEN RANK(K,I)=R(K,J)
780 NEXT J:NEXT I:NEXT K
790 RETURN
1000 DATA
9999,9999,64.4,103.9,157.3,9999,49.5,88.4,143.3,217.0,9999,62.6,112.3,182.4,276.2,9999,75.7,
136.1,221.4,335.2
1005 DATA 9999,88.7,159.9,260.2,394.15
1010 DATA 48.1,101.7,183.7,299.0,453.1,54,114.75,207.45,337.85,512.05
1015 DATA 60,127.8,231.2,376.7,571

1018 DATA 77.78,166.86,302.36,492.98,747.34
1019 DATA 83.8, 179.88,326.08,531.74,791.72
1020 DATA
89.8,192.9,349.8,570.5,864.9,95.8,205.92,373.54,609.28,923.66,101.76,218.94,397.28,648.06,9
82.42
1022 DATA 107.7,231.96,421.02,686.84,1041.18,113.82,244.98,444.76,725.62,1099.94
1030 DATA 119.7,258,468.5,764.4,1158.7

1060 DIM S1(21,8):FOR I=3 TO 20:FOR J=3 TO 7:READ S1(I,J):NEXT J:NEXT I

1100 DATA
9999,9999,75.6,122.8,185.6,9999,61.4,109.3,176.2,265,9999,80.5,142.8,229.4,343.8,9999,99.5,
176.1,282.4,422.6
1110 DATA
9999,75.95,118.45,209.4,335.35,501.25,66.8,137.4,242.7,388.3,579.9,75.9,156.35,275.9,441.15,
658.45
1120 DATA
85.1,175.3,309.1,494,737,94.28,194.2,342.32,546.84,815.5,103.46,213.1,375.54,599.68,894
1130 DATA
112.64,232,408.76,652.52,972.5,121.9,250.9,441.9,705.36,1051,131,269.8,475.2,758.2,1129.5
1140 DATA 140.2,
288.68,508.4,811,1207.98,149.4,307.56,541.6,863.8,1286.46,158.6,326.44,574.8,916.66,1364.9
4
1150 DATA 167.8,345.32,608,969.4,1443.42,177,364.2,641.2,1022.2,1521.9
1160 DIM S2(21,8):FOR I=3 TO 20:FOR J=3 TO 7:READ S2(I,J):NEXT J:NEXT I

1170 RETURN
```

```
2000 IF S<S1(M,N) THEN ?"P>0.05":STOP
2010 IF S=S1(M,N) THEN ?"P=0.05":STOP
2020 IF S>S1(M,N) AND S<S2(K,N) THEN ?"0.05>P>0.01":STOP
2030 IF S=S2(M,N) THEN ?"P=0.01":STOP
2040 IF S>S2(M,N) THEN ?"P<0.01":STOP

3000 DIM C(30):DIM D(30):DIM E(30)
3010 DATA
2.706,3.841,6.635,4.605,5.991,9.210,6.251,7.815,11.341,7.779,9.488,13.277,9.236,11.070,15.086
3020 DATA
10.645,12.592,16.812,12.017,14.067,18.475,13.362,15.507,20.090,14.684,16.919,21.666,15.987,
18.307,23.209
3030 DATA
17.275,19.675,24.725,18.549,21.026,26.217,19.812,22.362,27.688,21.064,23.685,29.141,22.307,
24.996,30.578
3040 DATA
23.542,26.296,32.000,24.769,27.587,33.409,25.989,28.869,34.805,27.204,30.144,36.191,28.41
2,31.410,37.566
3050 DATA
29.615,32.671,38.932,30.813,33.924,40.289,32.007,35.172,41.638,33.196,36.415,42.980,34.382,
37.652,44.314
3060 DATA
35.563,38.885,45.642,36.741,40.113,46.963,37.916,41.337,48.278,39.087,42.557,49.588,40.256,
43.773,50.892
3070 FOR I=1 TO 30
3080 READ C(I),D(I),E(I)
3090 NEXT I
3100 RETURN

4000 ?:?"H(0):";
4010 IF CHISQ=E(N-1) THEN ?"P=0.01":STOP
4020 IF CHISQ>E(N-1) THEN ?"P<0.01":STOP
4030 IF CHISQ=D(N-1) THEN ?"P=0.05":STOP
4040 IF CHISQ>D(N-1) THEN ?"0.05>P>0.01":STOP
4050 IF CHISQ=C(N-1) THEN ?"P=0.1":STOP
4060 IF CHISQ<C(N-1) THEN ?"P>0.1":STOP
4070 IFCHISQ>C(N-1) THEN ?"0.1>P>0.05":STOP
```

Print-out of the Kruskal-Wallis one-way Analysis of Variance test program

```
KRUSKAL_WALLIS - Notepad
File   Edit   Format   View   Help
10 REM KRUSKAL-WALLIS ONE WAY ANOVAR OF RANKS
20 GOSUB 3000:?"HOW MANY SAMPLES?";
30 INPUT M
40 ?
50 DIM Y(100,M+1):DIM G(100,M+1)
60 DIM M(100)
70 FOR C=1 TO M
80 ?"HOW MANY DATA IN SAMPLE";C
90 INPUT M(C)
100 ?
110 FOR I=1 TO M(C)
120 ?"ENTER DATUM";I;"SAMPLE";C
130 INPUT Y(I,C):G(I,C)=C
140 N=N+1
150 NEXT I
160 ?
170 NEXT C
180 DIM X(N)
190 DIM G1(N)
191 DIM Y1(N)
200 FOR I=1 TO M
210 FOR J=1 TO M(I)
220 K=K+1
230 X(K)=Y(J,I):G1(K)=G(J,I)
240 NEXT J
250 NEXT I
260 REM ORDER DATA
270 FOR J=1 TO N-1
280 FOR I=J TO N-1
290 IF X(J)<X(I+1) THEN 330
300 K=X(J):X=G1(J)
310 X(J)=X(I+1):G1(J)=G1(I+1)
320 X(I+1)=K:G1(I+1)=X
330 NEXT I
340 NEXT J
350 ?:?
360 DIM B(N+1):K=1
370 REM (FREQUENCY-1) OF GIVEN DATUM X(I) IN B(I)
380 FOR J=1 TO N-1
390 FOR I=J TO N-1
400 IF X(J)=X(I+1) THEN B(K)=B(K)+1
410 NEXT I:J=J+B(K):K=K+1
420 NEXT J
430 REM FREQUENCY OF GIVEN DATUM X(I) IN B(I)
440 FOR I=1 TO K:B(I)=B(I)+1:NEXT I
450 REM RANK DATA IN X(I) AND STORE RANKS IN R(I)
460 DIM R(N+1)
470 J=1
480 FOR I=1 TO K
490 IF B(I)>1 THEN 540
500 R(J)=J
```

```
510 J=J+1
520 NEXT I
530 GOTO 581
540 X=J
550 FOR J=X TO X+B(I)-1
560 R(J)=(X*B(I)+(B(I)^2-B(I))/2)/B(I)
570 NEXT J
580 GOTO 520
581 FOR I=1 TO N:FOR J=1 TO M:G(I,J)=0:NEXT J:NEXT I
590 K=1:?"RANKINGS BY SAMPLE":?:?
600 FOR I=1 TO M:?TAB(7*(I-1));I;:NEXT I
601 ?:?
1000 K=0:I=1
1005 FOR L=1 TO N
1010 FOR J=1 TO N
1020 IF (G1(J)<>999.999 AND G1(J)=I )THEN ?TAB(7*(I-1));R(J);:G(J,I)=R(J):G1(J)
=999.999:Y1(I)=Y1(I)+1:K=K+1:I=I+1:IF I=M+1 THEN I=1:?
1030 IF K=N THEN 1100
1035 IF Y1(I)=M(I) THEN I=I+1:IF I=M+1 THEN I=1:?
1037 IF Y1(I)=M(I) THEN 1010
1050 NEXT J
1055 IF L<N THEN NEXT L
1060 I=I+1:IF I=M+1 THEN I=1:?
1070 GOTO 1005
1100 ?:?:FOR I= 1 TO N:Y1(I)=0:NEXT I
1110 FOR I=1 TO M
1120 FOR J=1 TO N
1130 Y1(I)=Y1(I)+G(J,I)
1140 NEXT J
1150 NEXT I
1160 X=0
1170 FOR I=1 TO M
1180 X=X+Y1(I)^2/M(I)
1190 NEXT I
1200 X=X*12/(N*(N+1))-3*(N+1)
1210 ?"H=";X:?
1300 Y=0:FOR I=1 TO N
1310 Y=Y+B(I)^3-B(I)
1320 NEXT I
1330 H=X/(1-(Y/(N^3-N))):?"CORRECTED FOR TIES,  H=";H
1400 FOR I=1 TO M
1410 IF M(I)>5 THEN ?:? "DEGREES OF FREEDOM =";M-1:GOTO 4000
1420 NEXT I
1430 STOP

3000 DIM C(30):DIM D(30):DIM E(30)
3010 DATA
2.706,3.841,6.635,4.605,5.991,9.210,6.251,7.815,11.341,7.779,9.488,13.277,9.236,11.070,15.086
3020 DATA
10.645,12.592,16.812,12.017,14.067,18.475,13.362,15.507,20.090,14.684,16.919,21.666,15.987,
18.307,23.209
3030 DATA
17.275,19.675,24.725,18.549,21.026,26.217,19.812,22.362,27.688,21.064,23.685,29.141,22.307,
24.996,30.578
3040 DATA
23.542,26.296,32.000,24.769,27.587,33.409,25.989,28.869,34.805,27.204,30.144,36.191,28.41
2,31.410,37.566
```

```
3050 DATA
29.615,32.671,38.932,30.813,33.924,40.289,32.007,35.172,41.638,33.196,36.415,42.980,34.382,
37.652,44.314
3060 DATA
35.563,38.885,45.642,36.741,40.113,46.963,37.916,41.337,48.278,39.087,42.557,49.588,40.256,
43.773,50.892
3070 FOR I=1 TO 30
3080 READ C(I),D(I),E(I)
3090 NEXT I
3100 RETURN

4000 ?:?"H(0):";
4010 IF H=E(M-1) THEN ?"P=0.01":STOP
4020 IF H>E(M-1) THEN ?"P<0.01":STOP
4030 IF H=D(M-1) THEN ?"P=0.05":STOP
4040 IF (H>D(M-1) AND H<E(M-1)) THEN ?"0.05>P>0.01":STOP
4050 IF H=C(M-1) THEN ?"P=0.1":STOP
4060 IF H<C(M-1) THEN ?"P>0.1":STOP
4070 IF (H>C(M-1) AND H<D(M-1)) THEN ?"0.1>P>0.05":STOP
```

Friedman two-way Analysis of Variance for k Related Samples

```
100 GOSUB 3000:REM FRIEDMAN 2-WAY ANOVAR FOR MATCHED K-SAMPLE ORDINAL
DATA
250 ?"ENTER THE NUMBER DATA PER SAMPLE";
252 INPUT M
260 ?"ENTER THE NUMBER OF SAMPLES";
261 INPUT N
262 DIM SUM(N+1)
265 DIM B(M+1,N+1):DIM R(M+1,N+1)
270 DIM RANK (M+1,N+1):DIM Y(M+1,N+1)
312 DIM X(M+1,N+1)
313 FOR I=1 TO M
314 FOR J=1 TO N
315 ?"ENTER DATUM";I;"SAMPLE";J
316 INPUT X(I,J):Y(I,J)=X(I,J):NEXT J
317 NEXT I
320 FOR K=1 TO M:X=1:GOSUB 340:NEXT K
322 GOSUB 1000
324 FOR I=1 TO N
326 FOR J=1 TO M
328 SUM(I)=SUM(I)+RANK(J,I)
330 NEXT J:NEXT I
331 FOR J=1 TO N:CHISQUR=CHISQUR+SUM(J)^2
332 NEXT J:CHISQUR=(12/(M*N*(N+1)))*CHISQUR-3*M*(N+1)
333 ?"CHISQUARE=";CHISQUR;"ON",N-1;"DEGREES OF FREEDOM"
334 IF (M<=9 AND N=3) THEN STOP
335 IF (M<=4 AND N=4) THEN STOP
336 GOTO 4000
337 STOP
340 REM ORDER DATA
350 FOR J=1 TO N-1
360 FOR I=J TO N-1
370 IF X(K,J)<X(K,I+1) THEN 410
380 Y=X(K,J)
390 X(K,J)=X(K,I+1)
400 X(K,I+1)=Y
410 NEXT I
420 NEXT J
430 ?:?
450 REM
460 FOR J=1 TO N-1
470 FOR I=J TO N-1
480 IF X(K,J)=X(K,I+1) THEN B(K,X)=B(K,X)+1
490 NEXT I:J=J+B(K,X):X=X+1
500NEXT J
510 REM
520 FOR I=1 TO X:B(K,I)=B(K,I)+1:NEXT I
530 REM RANK DATA AND STORE IN R(I)
550 J=1
560 FOR I=1 TO X
570 IF B(K,I)>1 THEN 620
580 R(K,J)=J
590 J=J+1
600 NEXT I
601 RETURN
```

```
620 L=J
630 FOR J=L TO L+B(K,I)-1
640 R(K,J)=(L*B(K,I)+(B(K,I)^2-B(K,I))/2)/B(K,I)
650 NEXT J
660 GOTO 600
1000 FOR K=1 TO M
1010 FOR I=1 TO N
1020 FOR J=1 TO N
1030 IF Y(K,I)=X(K,J) THEN RANK(K,I)=R(K,J)
1040 NEXT J:NEXT I:NEXT K
1050 RETURN



3000 DIM C(30):DIM D(30):DIM E(30)
3010 DATA
2.706,3.841,6.635,4.605,5.991,9.210,6.251,7.815,11.341,7.779,9.488,13.277,9.236,11.070,15.086
3020 DATA
10.645,12.592,16.812,12.017,14.067,18.475,13.362,15.507,20.090,14.684,16.919,21.666,15.987,
18.307,23.209
3030 DATA
17.275,19.675,24.725,18.549,21.026,26.217,19.812,22.362,27.688,21.064,23.685,29.141,22.307,
24.996,30.578
3040 DATA
23.542,26.296,32.000,24.769,27.587,33.409,25.989,28.869,34.805,27.204,30.144,36.191,28.41
2,31.410,37.566
3050 DATA
29.615,32.671,38.932,30.813,33.924,40.289,32.007,35.172,41.638,33.196,36.415,42.980,34.382,
37.652,44.314
3060 DATA
35.563,38.885,45.642,36.741,40.113,46.963,37.916,41.337,48.278,39.087,42.557,49.588,40.256,
43.773,50.892
3070 FOR I=1 TO 30
3080 READ C(I),D(I),E(I)
3090 NEXT I
3100 RETURN

4000 ?:?"H(0):";
4010 IF CHISQUR=E(N-1) THEN ?"P=0.01":STOP
4020 IF CHISQUR>E(N-1) THEN ?"P<0.01":STOP
4030 IF CHISQUR=D(N-1) THEN ?"P=0.05":STOP
4040 IF (CHISQUR>D(N-1) AND CHISQUR<E(M-1)) THEN ?"0.05>P>0.01":STOP
4050 IF CHISQUR=C(N-1) THEN ?"P=0.1":STOP
4060 IF CHISQUR<C(N-1) THEN ?"P>0.1":STOP
4070 IF (CHISQUR>C(N-1) AND CHISQUR<D(M-1)) THEN ?"0.1>P>0.05":STOP
```

Print-out of the Randomization test for independent samples computer program

```
RANDOMIZATION - Notepad
File  Edit  Format  View  Help
5 REM FOR 2 INDEPENDENT SAMPLES AND INTERVAL DATA
10 ?"ENTER THE NUMBERS OF DATA IN THE LARGEST SAMPLE (OR EQUAL LARGEST)";
20 INPUT N
25 IF N=3 THEN ?"IF THE SIZE OF THE SECOND SAMPLE<3, NO OBTAINED DATA
COMBINATION COULD LEAD TO A REJECTION OF Ho  AT THE 0.05 LEVEL OR BEYOND. IF
THE SECOND SAMPLE SIZE =3, OBTAINED DATA COMBINATIONS OF THE 3 SMALLEST
DATA IN ONE SAMPLE LEAD TO A REJECTION OF Ho  AT THE 0.05 LEVEL":STOP
30 ?"ENTER THE NUMBER OF DATA IN THE SMALLEST (OR EQUAL SMALLEST) SAMPLE";
40 INPUT M
45 IF N+M>25 THEN ?"FOR TOTAL NUMBER OF DATA>25 USE THE 't' TEST":STOP

50 DIM Z(N+M+1): DIM A(M+1):DIM B(M+1):DIM C(M+1):DIM D(M+1):DIM E(M+1):DIM F
(M+1):DIM G(M+1):DIM H(M+1):DIM I(M+1):DIM J(M+1)
60 DIM K(M+1):DIM L(M+1):DIM M(M+1):DIM N(N+1):DIM O(M+1):DIM P(M+1):DIM Q
(M+1):DIM R(M+1):DIM S(M+1):DIM T(M+1):DIM U (M+1):DIM V(M+1):DIM W(M+1):DIM X
(M+1)
70 ?:?"ENTER THE DATA IN THE LARGEST SAMPLE (OR EQUAL LARGEST)"
80 FOR I=1 TO N:INPUT Z(I):Y=Y+Z(I):NEXT I
81 REM FIND THE SUM OF OBTAINED DATA IN THE LARGEST SAMPLE
90 ?:?"ENTER THE DATA IN THE SMALLEST SAMPLE (OR EQUAL SMALLEST)"
100 FOR I=N+1 TO N+M:INPUT Z(I):NEXT I
101 REM ARRAY Z(I) CONTAINS ALL THE DATA IN THE ORDER ENTERED
199 REM SORT THE DATA IN ASCENDING ORDER
200 FOR I=1 TO N+M-1
210 FOR J=I TO N+M-1
220 IF Z(I)>Z(J+1) THEN X=Z(I):Z(I)=Z(J+1):Z(J+1)=X
230 NEXT J:NEXT I
300 FOR I=1 TO M+1
301 ON N-3 GOTO
480,470,460,450,440,430,420,410,400,390,380,370,360,350,340,330,320,319,318,317,316
316 X(M+2-I)=Z(I+23)
317 W(M+2-I)=Z(I+22)
318 V(M+2-I)=Z(I+21)
319 U(M+2-I)=Z(I+20)
320 T(M+2-I)=Z(I+19)
330 S(M+2-I)=Z(I+18)
340 R(M+2-I)=Z(I+17)
350 Q(M+2-I)=Z(I+16)
360 P(M+2-I)=Z(I+15)
370 O(M+2-I)=Z(I+14)
380 N(M+2-I)=Z(I+13)
390 M(M+2-I)=Z(I+12)
400 L(M+2-I)=Z(I+11)
410 K(M+2-I)=Z(I+10)
420 J(M+2-I)=Z(I+9)
430 I(M+2-I)=Z(I+8)
440 H(M+2-I)=Z(I+7)
450 G(M+2-I)=Z(I+6)
460 F(M+2-I)=Z(I+5)
470 E(M+2-I)=Z(I+4)
```

```
480 D(M+2-I)=Z(I+3)
490 C(M+2-I)=Z(I+2)
500 B(M+2-I)=Z(I+1)
510 A(M+2-I)=Z(I)
520 NEXT I
524 X=0

1006
AA=1:BB=1:CC=1:DD=1:EE=1:FF=1:GG=1:HH=1:II=1:JJ=1:KK=1:LL=1:MM=1:NN=1:OO=1:PP=
1:QQ=1:RR=1:SS=1:TT=1:UU=1::VV=1:WW=1:XX=1:B1=1:C1=1:D1=1:E1=1:F1=1:G1=1:H1=1:I1=
1:J1=1:K1=1:L1=1:M1=1:N1=1:O1=1:P1=1:Q1=1:R1=1:S1=1:T1=1:U1=1:V1=1:W1=1:X1=1

1007 FOR X=XX TO M+1
1008 FOR W=WW TO M+1
1009 FOR V=VV TO M+1
1110 FOR U=UU TO M+1
1111 FOR T=TT TO M+1
1112 FOR S=SS TO M+1
1113 FOR R= RR TO M+1
1117 FOR Q=QQ TO M+1
1120 FOR P=PP TO M+1
1125 FOR O=OO TO M+1
1130 FOR NX=NN TO M+1
1135 FOR MX=MM TO M+1
1140 FOR L=LL TO M+1
1145 FOR K=KK TO M+1
1150 FOR J=JJ TO M+1
1155 FOR I=II TO M+1
1160 FOR H=HH TO M+1
1165 FOR G=GG TO M+1
1170 FOR F=FF TO M+1
1175 FOR E=EE TO M+1
1180 FOR D=DD TO M+1
1185 FOR C=CC TO M+1
1200 FOR B=BB TO M+1
1210 FOR A=AA TO M+1
1220 SUM = A(A)+B(B)+C(C)+D(D)+E(E)+F(F)+G(G)+H(H)+I(I)+J(J)+K(K)+L(L)+M(MX)+N
(NX)+O(O)+P(P)+Q(Q)+R(R)+S(S)+T(T)+U(U)+V(V)+W(W)+X(X)
1230 IF SUM>=Y THEN COUNT=COUNT+1
1240 NCR=NCR+1
1250 SUM=0
1260 NEXT A
1270 AA=AA+1:BB=BB+1
1280 NEXT B
1290 B1=B1+1:AA=B1:BB=B1
1300 NEXT C
1310 C1=C1+1:CC=CC+1:B1=C1:AA=C1:BB=C1
1320 NEXT D
1330 IF N=4 THEN GOTO 2000

1340 D1=D1+1:DD=DD+1:CC=D1:B1=D1:C1=D1:AA=D1:BB=D1

1350 NEXT E

1360 IF N=5 THEN GOTO 2000

1370 E1=E1+1:EE=EE+1:AA=E1:BB=E1:CC=E1:DD=E1:B1=E1:C12=E1:D1=E1
1380 NEXT F
1390 IF N=6 THEN 2000
```

```
1390 IF N=6 THEN 2000
1400 F1=F1+1:FF=FF+1:AA=F1:BB=F1:CC=F1:DD=F1:EE=F1:B1=F1:C1=F1:D1=F1:E1=F1
1410 NEXT G
1420 IF N=7 THEN GOTO 2000
1430
G1=G1+1:GG=GG+1:AA=G1:BB=G1:CC=G1:DD=G1:EE=G1:FF=G1:B1=G1:C1=G1:C1=G1:D1=
G1:E1=G1:F1=G1
1440 NEXT H
1450 IF N=8 THEN 2000

1460
H1=H1+1:HH=HH+1:AA=H1:BB=H1:CC=H1:DD=H1:EE=H1:FF=H1:GG=H1:B1=H1:C1=H1:D1=
H1:E1=H1:F1=H1:G1=H1
1470 NEXT I

1480 IF N=9 THEN 2000




1490
I1=I1+1:II=II+1:AA=I1:BB=I1:CC=I1:DD=I1:EE=I1:FF=I1:GG=I1:HH=I1:B1=I1:C1=I1:D1=I1:E1=I1:F
1=I1:G1=I1:H1=I1


1500 NEXT J
1510 IF N=10 THEN 2000
1520
J1=J1+1:JJ=JJ+1:AA=J1:BB=J1:CC=J1:DD=J1:EE=J1:FF=J1:GG=J1:HH=J1:II=J1:B1=J1:C1=J1:D1
=J1:E1=J1:F1=J1:G1=J1:H1=J1:I1=J1

1530 NEXT K

1540 IF N=11 THEN 2000

1550
K1=K1+1:KK=KK+1:AA=K1:BB=K1:CC=K1:DD=K1:EE=K1:FF=K1:GG=K1:HH=K1:II=K1:JJ=K1:
B1=K1:C1=K1:D1=K1:E1=K1:F1=K1:G1=K1:H1=K1:I1=K1:J1=K1
1555 NEXT L
1560 IF N=12 THEN 2000
1570
L1=L1+1:LL=LL+1:AA=L1:BB=L1:CC=L1:DD=L1:EE=L1:FF=L1:GG=L1:HH=L1:II=L1:JJ=L1:KK=L
1:B1=L1:C1=L1:D1=L1:E1=L1:F1=L1:G1=L1:H1=L1:I1=L1:J1=L1:K1=L1
1580 NEXT MX
1590 IF N=13 THEN 2000
1600
M1=M1+1:MM=MM+1:AA=M1:BB=M1:CC=M1:DD=M1:EE=M1:FF=M1:GG=M1:HH=M1:II=M1:
JJ=M1:KK=M1:LL=M1:B1=M1:C1=M1:D1=M1:E1=M1:F1=M1:G1=M1:H1=M1:I1=M1:J1=M1:K1=
M1:L1=M1
1610 NEXT NX
1620 IF N=14 THEN 2000
1630
N1=N1+1:NN=NN+1:AA=N1:BB=N1:CC=N1:DD=N1:EE=N1:FF=N1:GG=N1:HH=N1:II=N1:JJ=N
1:KK=N1:LL=N1:MM=N1:B1=N1:C1=N1:D1=N1:E1=N1:F1=N1:G1=N1:H1=N1:I1=N1:J1=N1:K1=
N1:L1=N1:M1=N1
1640 NEXT O
1650 IF N=15 THEN 2000
```

```
1660
O1=O1+1:OO=OO+1:AA=O1:BB=O1:CC=O1:DD=O1:EE=O1:FF=O1:GG=O1:HH=O1:II=O1:JJ
=O1:KK=O1:LL=O1:MM=O1:NN=O1:B1=O1:C1=O1:D1=O1:E1=O1:F1=O1:G1=O1:H1=O1:I1=
O1:J1=O1:K1=O1:L1=O1:M1=O1:N1=O1
1670 NEXT P
1680 IF N=16 THEN 2000


1690
P1=P1+1:PP=PP+1:AA=P1:BB=P1:CC=P1:DD=P1:EE=P1:FF=P1:GG=P1:HH=P1:II=P1:JJ=P1:KK
=P1:LL=P1:MM=P1:NN=P1:OO=P1:B1=P1:C1=P1:D1=P1:E1=P1:F1=P1:G1=P1:H1=P1:I1=P1:J1=
P1:K1=P1:L1=P1:M1=P1:N1=P1:O1=P1
1700 NEXT Q
1710 IF N=17 THEN 2000
1720
Q1=Q1+1:QQ=QQ+1:AA=Q1:BB=Q1:CC=Q1:DD=Q1:EE=Q1:FF=Q1:GG=Q1:HH=Q1:II=Q1:JJ
=Q1:KK=Q1:LL=Q1:MM=Q1:NN=Q1:OO=Q1:PP=Q1:B1=Q1:C1=Q1:D1=Q1:E1=Q1:F1=Q1:G1
=Q1:H1=Q1:I1=Q1:J1=Q1:K1=Q1:L1=Q1:M1=Q1:N1=Q1:O1=Q1:P1=Q1
1730 NEXT R
1740 IF N=18 THEN 2000

1750
R1=R1+1:RR=RR+1:AA=R1:BB=R1:CC=R1:DD=R1:EE=R1:FF=R1:GG=R1:HH=R1:II=R1:JJ=R1:KK
=R1:LL=R1:MM=R1:NN=R1:OO=R1:PP=R1:QQ=R1:B1=R1:C1=R1:D1=R1:E1=R1:F1=R1:G1=R1:
H1=R1:I1=R1:J1=R1:K1=R1:L1=R1:M1=R1:N1=R1:O1=R1:P1=R1:Q1=R1
1760 NEXT S

1770 IF N=19 THEN 2000
1780
S1=S1+1:SS=SS+1:AA=S1:BB=S1:CC=S1:DD=S1:EE=S1:FF=S1:GG=S1:HH=S1:II=S1:JJ=S1:KK
=S1:LL=S1:MM=S1:NN=S1:OO=S1:PP=S1:QQ=S1:RR=S1:B1=S1:C1=S1:D1=S1:E1=S1:F1=S1:
G1=S1:H1=S1:I1=S1:J1=S1:K1=S1:L1=S1:M1=S1:N1=S1:O1=S1:P1=S1:Q1=S1:R1=S1

1790 NEXT T

1800 IF N=20 THEN 2000
1810
T1=T1+1:TT=TT+1:AA=T1:BB=T1:CC=T1:DD=T1:EE=T1:FF=T1:GG=T1:HH=T1:II=T1:JJ=T1:KK
=T1:LL=T1:MM=T1:NN=T1:OO=T1:PP=T1:QQ=T1:RR=T1:SS=T1:B1=T1:C1=T1:D1=T1:E1=T1:
F1=T1:G1=T1:H1=T1:I1=T1:J1=T1:K1=T1:L1=T1:M1=T1:N1=T1:O1=T1:P1=T1:Q1=T1:R1=T1:S1=
T1

1820 NEXT U

1830 IF N=21 THEN 2000

1840
U1=U1+1:UU=UU+1:AA=U1:BB=U1:CC=U1:DD=U1:EE=U1:FF=U1:GG=U1:HH=U1:II=U1:JJ=U
1:KK=U1:LL=U1:MM=U1:NN=U1:OO=U1:PP=U1:QQ=U1:RR=U1:SS=U1:TT=U1:B1=U1:C1=U1
:D1=U1:E1=U1:F1=U1:G1=U1:H1=U1:I1=U1:J1=U1:K1=U1:L1=U1:M1=U1:N1=U1:O1=U1:P1=U
1:Q1=U1:R1=U1:S1=U1:T1=U1

1850 NEXT V
1860 IF N=22 THEN 2000
1870
V1=V1+1:VV=VV+1:AA=V1:BB=V1:CC=V1:DD=V1:EE=V1:FF=V1:GG=V1:HH=V1:II=V1:JJ=V1:
KK=V1:LL=V1:MM=V1:NN=V1:OO=V1:PP=V1:QQ=V1:RR=V1:SS=V1:TT=V1:UU=V1:B1=V1:C
1=V1:D1=V1:E1=V1:F1=V1:G1=V1:H1=V1:I1=V1:J1=V1:K1=V1:L1=V1:M1=V1:N1=V1:O1=V1:P1
=V1:Q1=V1:R1=V1:S1=V1:T1=V1:U1=V1
```

174

```
1880 NEXT W
1890 IF N=23 THEN 2000
1900
W1=W1+1:WW=WW+1:AA=W1:BB=W1:CC=W1:DD=W1:EE=W1:FF=W1:GG=W1:HH=W1:II=
W1:JJ=W1:KK=W1:LL=W1:MM=W1:NN=W1:OO=W1:PP=W1:QQ=W1:RR=W1:SS=W1:TT=W1:
UU=W1:VV=W1:B1=W1:C1=W1:D1=W1:E1=W1:F1=W1:G1=W1:H1=W1:I1=W1:J1=W1:K1=W1:
L1=W1:M1=W1:N1=W1:O1=W1:P1=W1:Q1=W1:R1=W1:S1=W1:T1=W1:U1=W1:V1=W1
1910 NEXT X




2000 ?:?"P (1 SIDED)";COUNT/NCR
2010 STOP
```

Print-out of the Randomization test for related samples

```
RANDOMIZATION_RM - Notepad
File  Edit  Format  View  Help
10 REM RANDOMIZATION TEST FOR 2 RELATED SAMPLES AND INTERVAL DATA
20 ?"HOW MANY PAIRS OF DATA?"
30 INPUT N:IF N>25 THEN STOP
35 DIM A(25):?"ENTER THE *difference* DATA FOR EACH MATCHED PAIR, WITH sign IF
NEGATIVE"
40 FOR I=1 TO N:INPUT A(I):Y=Y+A(I):A(I)=ABS(A(I)):NEXT I
42 REM
44 ON N -3 GOTO 290,270,250,
230,210,190,170,150,130,110,90,70,68,66,64,62,60,58,56,54,52,50
50 FOR Y1=1 TO 2
51 A(25)=-A(25)
52 FOR X1=1 TO 2
53 A(24)=-A(24)
54 FOR W1=1 TO 2
55 A(23)=-A(23)
56 FOR V1=V1 TO 2
57 A(22)=-A(22)
58 FOR U1=1 TO 2
59 A(21)=-A(21)
60 FOR T1=1 TO 2
61 A(20)=-A(20)
62 FOR S1=1 TO 2
63 A(19)=-A(19)
64 FOR R1=1 TO 2
65 A(18)=-A(18)
66 FOR Q1=1 TO 2
67 A(17)=-A(17)
68 FOR P1=1 TO 2
69 A(16)=-A(16)
70 FOR O1=1 TO 2
71 A(15)=-A(15)
90 FOR N1=1 TO 2
100 A(14)=-A(14)
110 FOR M1=1 TO 2
120 A(13)=-A(13)
130 FOR L1=1 TO 2
140 A(12)=-A(12)
150 FOR K1=1 TO 2
160 A(11)=-A(11)
170 FOR J1=1 TO 2
180 A(10)=-A(10)
190 FOR I1=1 TO 2
200 A(9)=-A(9)
210 FOR H1=1 TO 2
220 A(8)=-A(8)
230 FOR G1=1 TO 2
240 A(7)=-A(7)
250 FOR F1=1 TO 2
260 A(6)=-A(6)
270 FOR E1=1 TO 2
280 A(5)=-A(5)
290 FOR D1=1 TO 2
300 A(4)=-A(4)
310 FOR C1=1 TO 2
```

176

```
320 A(3)=-A(3)
330 FOR B1=1 TO 2
340 A(2)=-A(2)
350 FOR A1=1 TO 2
360 A(1)=-A(1)
370 FOR ZZ=1 TO N:SUM=SUM+A(ZZ):NEXT ZZ
380 IF SUM>=Y THEN COUNT=COUNT+1
390 SUM=0:X=X+1:REM X COMBINATIONS
400 NEXT A1:NEXT B1:NEXT C1:NEXT D1
410 IF N=4 THEN 1000
420 NEXT E1
430 IF N= 5 THEN 1000
440 NEXT F1
450 IF N= 6 THEN 1000
460 NEXT G1
470 IF N= 7 THEN 1000
480 NEXT H1
490 IF N= 8 THEN 1000
500 NEXT I1
510 IF N= 9 THEN 1000
520 NEXT J1
530 IF N= 10 THEN 1000
540 NEXT K1
550 IF N= 11 THEN 1000
560 NEXT L1
570 IF N= 12 THEN 1000
580 NEXT M1
590 IF N= 13 THEN 1000
600 NEXT N1
610 IF N= 14 THEN 1000
620 NEXT O1
630 IF N= 15 THEN 1000
640 NEXT P1
650 IF N= 16 THEN 1000
660 NEXT Q1
670 IF N= 17 THEN 1000
680 NEXT R1
690 IF N= 18 THEN 1000
700 NEXT S1
710 IF N= 19 THEN 1000
720 NEXT T1
730 IF N= 20 THEN 1000
740 NEXT U1
750 IF N= 21 THEN 1000
760 NEXT V1
770 IF N= 22 THEN 1000
780 NEXT W1
790 IF N= 23 THEN 1000
800 NEXT X1
810 IF N= 24 THEN 1000

1000 ?"P (1-SIDED)=";COUNT/X
```

Print-out of the Mode calculating program

```
MODE - Notepad
File  Edit  Format  View  Help
10 REM CALCULATES MODE
20 ?"ENTER THE NUMBER OF DATA"
30 INPUT N
40 DIM X(N+1)
50 FOR I=1 TO N
60 ?"ENTER DATUM";I;
70 INPUT X(I):SUM=SUM+X(I)
80 NEXT I
90 FOR J=1 TO N-1
100 FOR I=J TO N-1
110 IF X(J)<X(I+1) THEN 150
120 K=X(J)
130 X(J)=X(I+1)
140 X(I+1)=K
150 NEXT I
160 NEXT J
170 ?:?
180 ?"RANKED DATA:"
190 ?
200 FOR I=1 TO N
210 ? X(I);
220 NEXT I
230 ?:?
240 IF (N/2)-N/2<0 THEN MEDIAN=X(INT(N/2)+1):GOTO 360
340 MEDIAN=(X(INT(N/2))+X(INT(N/2)+1))/2
350 ?:?
360 DIM B(N+1):DIM Z(N+1):K=1
370 FOR J=1 TO N-1
380 FOR I=J TO N-1
390 IF X(J)=X(I+1) THEN B(K)=B(K)+1
400 NEXT I:Z(K)=X(J):J=J+B(K):K=K+1
410 NEXT J
420 FOR I=1 TO K-1
430 IF B(1)>B(I+1) THEN 500
440 C=B(1)
450 D=Z(1)
460 B(1)=B(I+1)
470 Z(1)=Z(I+1)
480 B(I+1)=C
490 Z(I+1)=d
500 NEXT I
510 IF B(1)=0 THEN ?"NO MODE":GOTO 670
520 C=1:X(1)=Z(1)
530 FOR I=1 TO K-1
540 IF (B(1)=B(I+1)) THEN X(C+1)=Z(I+1):C=C+1
550 NEXT I
555 IF C=1 THEN 640



560 FOR J=1 TO C-1
570 FOR I=J TO C-1
```

```
580 IF X(J)<X(I+1) THEN 620
590 K=X(J)
600 X(J)=X(I+1)
610 X(I+1)=K
620 NEXT I
630 NEXT J
640 ?"MODE:"
650 FOR I=1 TO C:? X(I);" ";
660 NEXT I
670 ?:?:?"MEDIAN:":? MEDIAN

680 ?"MEAN:":?SUM/N
```

Print-out of the Histogram Extension to the Mode calculating program

```
690 STOP
1000 ?"OF THE HISTOGRAM:":?
1010 ?"ENTER THE CLASS INTERVAL";
1020 INPUT I
1025 ?"ENTER THE LOWER BOUNDARY OF MODAL CLASS";
1027 INPUT XL

1030 ?"ENTER THE FREQUENCY OF THE MODAL CLASS";
1040 INPUT FM
1050 ?"ENTER THE FREQUENCY OF THE CLASS TO THE left OF THE MODAL CLASS";
1060 INPUT FL
1070 ?"ENTER THE FREQUENCY OF THE CLASS TO THE right OF THE MODAL CLASS";
1075 INPUT FR

1080 MODE = XL+(FM-FL)*I/(2*FM-FR-FL)
1090 ?"MODE (estimated):":?INT(MODE+.5)
```

Print-out of the Skewness calculating program

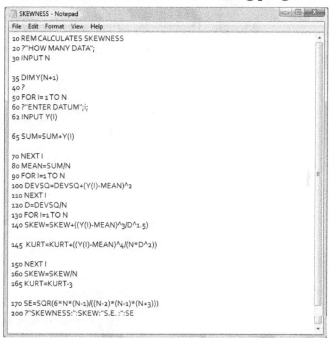

```
SKEWNESS - Notepad
File  Edit  Format  View  Help
10 REM CALCULATES SKEWNESS
20 ?"HOW MANY DATA";
30 INPUT N

35 DIM Y(N+1)
40 ?
50 FOR I=1 TO N
60 ?"ENTER DATUM";i;
62 INPUT Y(I)

65 SUM=SUM+Y(I)

70 NEXT I
80 MEAN=SUM/N
90 FOR I=1 TO N
100 DEVSQ=DEVSQ+(Y(I)-MEAN)^2
110 NEXT I
120 D=DEVSQ/N
130 FOR I=1 TO N
140 SKEW=SKEW+((Y(I)-MEAN)^3/D^1.5)

145 KURT=KURT+((Y(I)-MEAN)^4/(N*D^2))

150 NEXT I
160 SKEW=SKEW/N
165 KURT=KURT-3

170 SE=SQR(6*N*(N-1)/((N-2)*(N-1)*(N+3)))
200 ?"SKEWNESS:":SKEW:"S.E. :":SE
```

Print-out of the Kurtosis Extension to the Skewness calculating program

```
145 KURT=KURT+((Y(I)-MEAN)^4/(N*D^2))

150 NEXT I
160 SKEW=SKEW/N
165 KURT=KURT-3

170 SE=SQR(6*N*(N-1)/((N-2)*(N-1)*(N+3)))
200 ?"SKEWNESS:";SKEW;"S.E. :";SE
210 ?"KURTOSIS:";KURT;"S.E.:";SQR(24*N*(N-1)^2/((N-2)*(N-3)*(N+5)*(N+3)))
```

180

BIBLIOGRAPHY & RERERENCES

et
Alcock, D. (1981) *Illustrating BASIC* Cambridge University Press, Cambridge

Daly, F., Hand, D., Jones, M. Lunn, A. and McConway, K. (1995) *Elements of Statistics* Addison-Wesley

Graham, G. and Graham, C. (1988) *G.C.S.E. Mathematics Revise* Charles Letts & Co Ltd

Friedman (1937) 'The use of ranks to avoid the assumption of normality implicit in the analysis of variance' *J.Amer.Stats*,**32**, pp. 675-701

(1999) *Ti-83 Graphics Calculator* Texas Instruments

(2013) *YouGov/Sunday Times Results* http://ww.yougov.com   (accessed 14/6/2013)

181

Kopnicky, L. (2011) *Vintage BASIC*
http://www.vintage-basic.net
(accessed 14/12/2011)

Neave, H. (1991) *Elementary Statistics Tables*
Routledge, London

Piaget, J., Inhelder, B. and Szeminska, A. (1960)
The Child's Conception of Geometry Routledge
and Kegan Paul

Siegel, S. (1956) *Nonparametric Statistics for the Behavioral Sciences* McGraw-Hill

(1999) *Texas Instruments TI-83 Plus*

(2003) *Minitab Student Release 14*

(1997) *Genstat 5 Third edition Student Version* Lawes Agricultural Trust, Rothampstead

182

Trigger, P. (1985) *An investigation into the Mathematics attainments of the Hearing-Impaired* Unpublished Ph.D Thesis, University of London, Institute of Education

Trigger, P. (2013a) *Wind Turbines: Description, Appraisal & Alternatives* Amazon Kindle Publishing.

Vols. I-IV:

ISBN 9781494252137

ISBN 9781494252120

ISBN 9781494481209

ISBN 1494481219

Trigger P. (2013b) *The Generation and Transmission of Electricity: A Historical View* Amazon Kindle Publishing

ISBN 194319349

www.ingramcontent.com/pod-product-compliance
Lightning Source LLC
Chambersburg PA
CBHW071154050326

40689CB00011B/2106